MEL TH

GW00871471

Leading

THE Way

VOLUME I

Hodder & Stoughton

LONDON SYDNEY AUCKLAND TORONTO

Acknowledgements

The Publishers would like to thank the following for permission to reproduce material in this volume:

Darton, Longman and Todd Ltd/The Anglican Book Centre for the extracts from *The Broken Body* by Jean Vanier (1988); Darton, Longman and Todd Ltd/Novalis for the extract from *The Challenge of l'Arche* by Jean Vanier (1982); Friends of the Earth for 'What You Can Do' from *Water Pollution in Britain*; Hodder and Stoughton Ltd for the extracts from *Which One's Cliff?* and *Single Minded* both by Cliff Richard; Newspaper Publishing Plc for the Map of Oxleas Wood by William Brown from *The Independent*, 22 July, 1989; Nipponzan Myohoji for the material from *Peace Pagoda*; Barrie and Jenkins for the extracts from *As It Happens* by Jimmy Savile (1974).

Every effort has been made to trace and acknowledge ownership of copyright. The publishers will be glad to make suitable arrangements with any copyright holders whom it has not been possible to contact.

The Publishers would also like to thank the following for their permission to reproduce copyright photographs in this book:

Sue Andrews – pp 4, 9, 10; L'Arche – pp85, 87t a b, 88, 89, 91; J Allan Cash – p81; Cephas Picture Library – p59; CND – pp61, 63; Environmental Picture Library – pp26, 27, 30; Format Partners – p44; Friends of the Earth – pp22, 24; Chris Gitter FoE – p29; The Guardian/Ian Swift – pp76, 79; Hulton Picture Company – p51; The Independen Peter McDiarmid – p28; Roshini Kempadoo – pp42, 43; Jeni McKenzie – pp12, 15, 16, 17t and b NASA – p23; The Pilsdon Community – p36; Popperfoto – p56; The Cliff Richard Organisatio pp5, 6; Chris Schwarz – pp66, 67, 68, 69, 72; Max Sinclair – p54; St Christopher's Hospice – pp70, 7 and b; Stoke Mandeville Hospital – p55; Tear Fu – p7; Mel Thompson – pp32, 35, 58, 64; Topham Picture Source – pp13, 50, 52, 60.

British Library Cataloguing in Publication Data
Thompson, M. R. (Melvyn Rodney) *1946*
   Leading the way.
   1 Social problems. Christian viewpoints
   I. Title
   261.83

   ISBN 0–340–51955–X Vol. 1
   ISBN 0–340–52347–6 Vol. 2

   ISBN 0 340 51955 X

First published 1991

© 1991 Mel Thompson

All rights reserved. No part of this publication may be reproduced or transmitted in any form or by any means, electronic or mechanical, including photocopy, recording, or any information storage and retrieval system, without permission in writing from the publisher or under licence from the Copyright Licensing Agency Limited. Further details of such licences (for reprographic reproduction) may be obtained from the Copyright Licensing Agency Limited, of 33–34 Alfred Place, London WC1E 7DP.

Typeset by Gecko Ltd, Bicester
Printed in Great Britain for the eductional publishing division of Hodder and Stoughton Ltd, Mill Road, Dunton Green, Sevenoaks, Kent by Thomson Litho Ltd, East Kilbride

Contents

Introduction

Leading the Way looks at personal, social and religious issues through the eyes of those who are involved in them. Each chapter features someone whose beliefs and convictions about life have led him or her to a commitment to help others – by doing something practical for those in need, by raising money or working for charities, or by promoting their religious beliefs. They give their own comments, showing what is most important for them, and how they came to be involved.

Some of the people in this book are well known, others are not; some have started new organisations, others work within those started by other people; but they are all equally leading the way. For each of them, their life and work has been changed because of something about which they feel strongly. Leading the way is not reserved for the famous, it is for everyone.

To the teacher

The chapters in *Leading the Way* have been compiled from interviews with, or material published by, the people featured. Each chapter therefore represents a personal statement, rather than an objective assessment, although some background information has been included in order to help pupils to understand the issues with which these people are concerned. The book is intended to be a basis for further reflection and discussion, as well as an introduction to some of the most important personal, social and religious issues of our day.

Implicit in the chapters – and drawn out in some of the 'Over to you' assignments – is the idea of leading the way. All the people featured have found that their way of life has been challenged and changed by responding to some practical, moral or religious conviction. Some are leading a way of life very different from that which they imagined when they were younger. Some have led the way by setting up new organisations or ventures. Others have become spokespersons for great issues. Not all of them are well known – which may serve to show pupils that they too may be challenged to 'lead the way'.

All the major world relgions have the idea of 'the way' that people are to follow – a way based on moral and religious convictions, in contrast to a life of aimless drifting. Some of those featured in *Leading the Way* speak about their religious beliefs, others do not, but all illustrate a sense of purpose and direction in life – a direction which provides the context within which religious and moral ideas make sense, and which can show their relevance.

Cliff Richard

LIVING AS A CHRISTIAN POP SINGER

> 66 *Very simply I say to God, 'Here is my art form; I'll perform it to the best of my ability, I'll try not to bring dishonour on you; please use it and let any glory that's going be for yourself.* 99

Can someone be a Christian and also earn large sums of money in show business? How should a person's religion influence his or her career?

Cliff Richard is a Christian pop singer who is prepared to speak out about his religious faith. After more than thirty years in the pop business, and having thought at one time that he should give it all up and become an RE teacher, he believes that he can best serve God through his music.

Cliff Richard supports TEAR Fund, a Christian charity providing aid and development for some of the world's poorest people. He admires the work of doctors, nurses and relief workers, but he couldn't do that sort of work himself. Instead, he raises money through Gospel concerts, to provide for those with the practical skills to help.

He is also involved with the Christian Arts Centre, where musicians, artists and people from the theatre gather to share their faith and to support one another.

Cliff Richard was born in India in 1940. At that time, India was still part of the British Empire, and most British people in India lived in comfort. Cliff's family had servants to cook and clean for them, and he remembers being happy there as a child. They all went to church (and Cliff sang in the choir), but it was a social event and a chance to meet other people, not like the commitment to Christianity that Cliff made later in life. Then, as India prepared to become independent in 1947, there was rioting, and it was not safe for them to stay, so his family moved back to Britain.

When they arrived in England, they were poor. From a life of luxury with servants, Cliff, his parents and his three sisters found themselves having to share a room in a relative's house in North London. Eventually they

" Life was fabulous. At twenty-one, I was being paid for the only thing I ever wanted to do, the fans were screaming, and career-wise I had it made. Endless opportunities in films, television and recording were opening up. If it was lonely at the top, I couldn't imagine why; around me were people I liked, friends I worked with, and family I loved and lived with.

And then, very very faintly, something inside said –

Please, I'm not satisfied.
"

managed to get a council house, but they had little furniture and not enough money to live on.

When he was at school, Cliff showed no particular interest in religion. He wasn't keen on school anyway. What really excited him was rock'n'roll, and he loved the music of Elvis Presley. From the age of fourteen, rock music seemed the most important thing in his life, and he formed a group to sing at the local youth club.

When he left school, Cliff took an ordinary office job, which he found boring. His real interest was in singing, which he did in the evenings and at weekends. His first group was called The Drifters. They played at local youth clubs, Saturday night dances and pubs in the area of Cheshunt and Waltham Cross, where Cliff lived. Quickly they were in demand, and within a year Cliff had signed a recording contract. Like many other people in the entertainment world, he decided to change his name, so he stopped being called Harry Webb – the name with which he was born – and became Cliff Richard. In August 1958 he left his office job and started life as a professional pop musician.

He quickly achieved success, and by his eighteenth birthday he was well established, with Cliff Richard and The Drifters (they later changed their name to The Shadows). Suddenly he found himself with television and stage shows, recordings and films.

Cliff performing with The Shadows, 1960

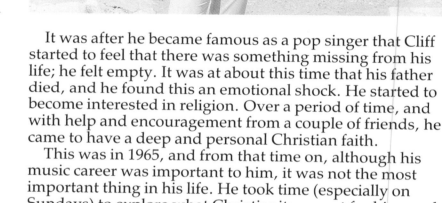

Cliff in the film Summer Holiday. It was a time of success for him, but also a time when he started to ask questions about the real meaning and purpose of his life.

66 *When I was prepared to give the career up, God said, 'Don't, we'll use it.'* 99

It was after he became famous as a pop singer that Cliff started to feel that there was something missing from his life; he felt empty. It was at about this time that his father died, and he found this an emotional shock. He started to become interested in religion. Over a period of time, and with help and encouragement from a couple of friends, he came to have a deep and personal Christian faith.

This was in 1965, and from that time on, although his music career was important to him, it was not the most important thing in his life. He took time (especially on Sundays) to explore what Christianity meant for him, and he tried to work out how to combine it with his life as a pop star. He was involved with Crusaders – Christian youth groups – where he eventually became a leader, helping with outings and summer camps. He also appeared at the 'Youth Night' at a Billy Graham rally in 1966. For someone as well known as Cliff Richard, there was no hiding the fact that he had become a Christian.

For some time, Cliff wondered if he should change his career and become a teacher. He worked in his spare time to take an O level (like a GCSE) in RE, set about ending his fan club, and started to make it known that he was quitting showbusiness.

At that time, without him trying at all, several opportunities came his way – including religious television shows. He realised that it would be better for him to use opportunities like this in the service of Christ, rather than give it all up.

TEAR Fund

In 1969 Cliff Richard gave the first of many concerts which have been arranged to support the charity TEAR Fund. This is a Christian organisation, set up in 1968, which gives relief and development aid to those who are suffering in the countries of the Third World, whether through absolute poverty and starvation or through some natural disaster.

TEAR Fund stands for **T**he **E**vangelical **A**lliance **R**elief Fund. The Evangelical Alliance is an organisation set up by Christians who think that it is particularly important to preach about their faith. TEAR Fund provides both money and people to help national churches, missionary societies and other Christian groups. In emergencies, it sends food and medical supplies to those in need, but much of its work is to enable local Christians to help to develop health care, water supplies, agriculture and the other things that are needed for the people in their areas. TEAR Fund also supports Christian education and evangelism (preaching about Christ), and some Christians in Britain are encourged to sponsor individual children in the Third World, helping them with money, and also getting to know them.

This way of working appealed to Cliff because it both offered practical help to the people and also spread the message of Christ. Those who support TEAR Fund see it as 'love in action' – a practical expression of their concern for people, showing their Christian commitment.

These children are being helped by TEAR Fund at a refugee camp in Thailand.

On his way back from a concert in Australia, Cliff visited Bangladesh to see something of the TEAR Fund projects there. He walked around one of the refugee camps, horrified by the starvation and suffering he saw there – so soon after the luxury and comfort of Australia.

Cliff feels that, even though the situation sometimes seems hopeless and the number of people needing help so vast, it is still important to do whatever is possible. But what could a rock musician do? A nurse helped him find the answer.

66 *Everyone in those camps, even the babies, were covered in sores and scabs. I was bending down to one little mite, mainly for the photographer's benefit, and trying hard not to have too close a contact, when someone accidentally stood on the child's fingers. He screamed out and, as a reflex, I grabbed hold of him, forgetting all about his dirt and his sores. I remember now that warm little body clinging to me and the crying instantly stopped. In that moment I knew I had an enormous amount to learn about practical Christian loving but that at least I'd started.* 99

Can you give an injection?

No way; I'd never have the nerve.

Then go home. We don't need you here. Go back and do what you're good at.

As part of his work for TEAR Fund, Cliff gives Gospel concerts in order to raise money – already more than half a million pounds. He is not a doctor or a nurse, who could give direct help to those who are suffering, but he is able to use his particular gift of music to help finance those who can. He also helped to make a film about the work of TEAR Fund, called *Cliff in Kenya*.

But helping those who are suffering in the Third World is not just a matter of giving. Cliff says:

66 *My twenty year association with the Christian relief and development agency, TEAR Fund, has given me far more than I've been able to contribute. In terms of understanding and sorting out personal priorities, my trips to Third World countries – such as Haiti, Bangladesh and Sudan – have been invaluable.* 99

A photo of Cliff with the little boy he helped in the refugee camp hangs on the wall between his bedroom and bathroom, where he can't fail to see it or remember it.

Helping those in need gives you a new way of thinking about yourself and the things that you have. The top 30 per cent of the world's population have 80 per cent of the world's wealth. Cliff Richard, who is able to earn large sums of money through his work, sees that sharing it with those in need is important for him and expresses his Christian commitment.

A Christian in show business

Increasingly, after he became a Christian, Cliff Richard found himself accepting invitations to attend services, meetings and Crusader classes. He would sing and give his personal testimony. He soon found that he was not good as a preacher, but was far better at answering questions, so he often chose to appear as one half of a dialogue, talking freely about his faith. At first he appeared mainly at church services or in Crusader class, singing two or three Gospel songs and speaking about his faith. Later he found himself invited to all kinds of gatherings, sometimes in churches and cathedrals, but sometimes in universities at the invitation of groups of Christian students.

One of the ways in which Cliff shares his faith is through writing. Here he signs copies of one of his books.

Sometimes he includes a song with a religious theme in his stage shows, but he insists that it must still be good music – he won't sing a poor song just because it's religious. There is a danger that including any religious song may offend some people – but he does it because he refuses to keep his faith and his work separate. He believes that everything can influence people, and he is determined to use his own public image and communication for the service of Christ.

Cliff Richard was awarded an OBE (Order of the British Empire medal) in 1980, and his success in the entertainment world has been massive, with over a hundred recordings, including thirteen gold and thirty-five silver discs. Even after thirty years in the pop world, he is able to get to number one in the charts for an album, a single, a CD and a video simultaneously.

This is amazing when you think that most performers are popular for just a few years, or sometimes just a matter of months. With films, stage shows, rock tours and television appearances as well as his recordings and videos, his life is packed with work. Yet he still finds time for his charity and Christian commitments.

> 66 *To my mind, everything we do on stage as artists is done to achieve some kind of effect. If I'm singing a love song, I want to affect people emotionally; if it's a song about pollution, I want them to think, 'Ugh, he's right'; if they are Jesus lyrics, then I'd like people to know that I believe them. Each song communicates in its own way and, if there were no effect, I wouldn't waste time singing it.* 99

As with all performers, there have been times when some people have criticised his style of music, or the kind of television programmes that he has done, but Cliff has just continued to do what he believes to be right. He is a professional and a perfectionist – everything that he does has to be as good as possible – but still his first priority is his Christian faith, and the support he gives to those in need.

Over to you

1 Imagine that you are a well-known pop singer, and that you have become a committed member of a religion.
   - What problems might you face in taking part in worship and in the activities of those who share your faith?
   - What special opportunities might you work offer you?

2 Collect together some information about TEAR Fund and the way in which it works.
   - How important do you think it is for people to share their beliefs with those they are trying to help?
   - List the skills that may be used in relief work in the Third World. Then list those skills that are not directly connected with aid, but which could be used to help the helpers.
   - Cliff Richard says that he has gained a great deal from his experience of seeing the work of TEAR Fund. What do you think he means by this? Put in your own words the way in which seeing those who are poor can help a wealthy person sort out his or her priorities.
   - Can you name any other charities which give aid to people in the Third World?

3 Imagine that you are an actor or actress, and you are offered an important part in a play. You look through the script and find that some of the things you are going to be expected to say on stage go against your religious beliefs. What should you do?

4 Some pop songs (like Cliff's 'Mistletoe and Wine') come out at Christmas time and have a theme connected with Christmas. But right through the year, pop songs include words which have some religious meaning – whether they are about love, or peace, or forgiving one another. Make a collection of the words of pop songs which have a religious meaning.

Address for further information about TEAR Fund –

TEAR Fund
100 Church Road
Teddington
Middlesex   TW11 8QE

You may apply to the Resources Department for a pack of information for secondary schools.

For those wanting to find out more about Cliff Richard and his Christian views, his books include a recent biography, *Single Minded* (1988) and his religious views are also expressed in *You, Me and Jesus* (1985), *Jesus, Me and You* (1988) and *Mine Forever* (1989) – all of which are published by Hodder & Stoughton.

Sybil Phoenix

HELPING YOUNG PEOPLE OF ALL RACES

Sybil Phoenix has spent her whole working life helping young people in different ways. She is particularly concerned about the needs of young West Indians living in Britain, and feels that it is important for them to learn about the countries from which they have come. Having experienced racial prejudice herself, she has worked to improve race relations. She was the founder of the Moonshot Youth and Community Centre in South-East London, runs a house for girls who are away from home and in need of care, and has fostered more children than she can remember!

66 *I call myself 'Big Youth, because I've spent all my life representing young people and working with them.* **99**

66 *Fostering children has been hard work, but it has also been a lot of joy.* **99**

Sybil Phoenix was born in Guyana, a country on the north-east coast of South America. She was an active member of her local Methodist church, and became involved in youth work. She trained as a social worker – which, at that time, meant that she had to deal with the problems of all kinds of people, both young and old.

In 1951 she came to Britain, and settled in South-East London, with her husband Joe. At that time, the British government was advertising in Guyana and elsewhere for people to come to and live in Britain, for there was a shortage of labour. It was not long after the Second World War, industry was expanding again, and there was a desperate need for more people to run public transport.

To start with, Sybil Phoenix registered as a child-minder, working with babies and toddlers in a day nursery. She also started running a youth and community centre, but found that the British authorities did not accept the qualification in social work that she had gained in Guyana, so she had to start all over again and take another training course. It was a very hard time for her, trying to keep pace with both her training and her other work.

The 1950s saw the first multi-racial bus crews in Britain. The government advertised for people to come and live in Britain because of a shortage of labour.

66 *I've always been a Sunday School teacher and youth worker within the Church. When I came to Britain, the minister of the church back in Guyana gave me a letter, and also wrote to the local church here so that we could be in touch. It wasn't long before the local minister found me.* 99

She soon became involved with a local church when she arrived in Britain, setting up a choir for children, and doing youth work. Both in the Church and in the community, Sybil Phoenix found that people came to her with their problems. She has a natural way of showing sympathy, and also has the energy to help them and to offer advice. Fortunately, her professional position as a social worker was exactly what suited her personality, and although she found it exhausting, she enjoyed her work.

Although she has now officially retired as a church worker in the Methodist Church, she is still actively involved in a multi-racial ministry. She sees her Christian faith as the basis on which her whole view of life and her commitment to helping people have been built.

As well as bringing up her own children, and working with young people in the community through youth clubs and other organisations, Sybil Phoenix has fostered so many children that she has lost count of how many have stayed with her!

Moonshot Youth Club

Sybil Phoenix was asked to take over the running of a local youth club, which was mainly used by West Indians. She went along to look at it.

We want a disco every night!

They ought to do something more than that!

13

She insisted that, if she were to take over, the children should do something educational as well as entertaining. In particular, she felt that they should learn about the West Indies, and she also wanted games to be provided for them. To her surprise, it was agreed that she could do this, and a hut was hired in which she could run these other activities.

> 66 *All I saw was a couple of hundred young people in a darkened room playing music, and I said I wasn't prepared to do that!* 99

Where do you go after school?

We just play around in the streets, until our parents tell us to get home.

She wanted to organise more things for them, but did not have enough help. Then, after three children were killed in road accidents locally, she was given two extra workers to help with the club.

Some children were having difficulty with their work at school. She thought that they would be better off if they followed the routine that she had known as a child – so she set about providing homework, to keep them occupied and help them to make progress. At first the teachers were confused by this.

> 66 *At home I was trained that, when you come home from school, you had some lemonade and a bun or biscuit and then you did your homework before you went out to play.* 99

Who set you this homework?

But as they learned more about Sybil Phoenix, she started to be invited into schools. She found that teachers were ignorant about the West Indies, and were therefore unable to teach their pupils about the place and the culture from which they and their parents had come, so she set about putting this right and teaching about West Indian life. She believes that it is vitally important that people should know their roots – should understand the history of their own people – otherwise they will not feel that they belong anywhere.

The Pagnell Street Centre offers a range of sporting and other activities for people of all ages.

66 *A tree without its roots is no tree at all, and people who have no roots will always tend to blow around in the wind.* **99**

The youth club became known as the Moonshot Youth Club – it ran a successful disco and became an important centre for young West Indians. At one stage the club was destroyed in a fire, but she was determined that it would open up again, and she herself raised nearly £100,000 towards the project. As a result of her efforts, the Pagnell Street Centre was built.

Although the earlier club had concentrated mainly on the needs of young West Indians, the new community centre is able to cater for people of all races, and to provide a wide variety of opportunities for them. In this way, the centre hopes to help break down barriers between people of different racial groups.

Some people use the centre for sports – its programme includes badminton, football, gymnastics and weightlifting. Others come for educational classes – learning the basic skills of reading, writing and mathematics, or taking classes in needlework or first aid.

For many people, the centre is a place where they can meet and offer support to one another. One example of this is the Black Women's Group, where women from different professional backgrounds can meet. They raise funds to help young people, and also organise a baby-sitting circle, so that those with children can get out of the home in the evenings. There is also a Young Mothers' Project, which provides a crèche for their children and organises various activities and outings. An important feature of the centre is that there is generally someone available to give help and advice to those who have problems.

Living in a city

In helping young people, Sybil Phoenix has become involved with the problems of all those who live in busy inner-city areas. It can be lonely in a city, especially if you are in a flat high up in a block, where you cannot see your neighbours. Going to a youth club or community centre is one way of overcoming these problems – by making friends, feeling that you really belong to your local community, and learning something useful to improve the quality of your life.

Life in her part of South-East London has changed a lot since the 1950s. When Sybil Phoenix first arrived, there were no tall blocks of flats, just rows of small houses. The people were also rather different from today.

It can be lonely living in a flat high up in one of these blocks.

In those days, many of the black families had never crossed the water.

What do you mean?

They didn't yet feel that they belonged in Britain. They had never seen Buckingham Palace, or other famous places, although they lived quite close to them.

> ❝ *Most of that has gone now, the area has changed. Today people have more money.* ❞

Some of the poorest people used to spend their weekends at railway stations, begging. They would also go to the fruit and vegetable markets and gather up the food that was thrown out, or that had been left behind by the traders, some of it still good. There were families where the menfolk were in and out of prison, and the women had to cope as best they could.

At one time she met people who lived in very bad conditions; their houses had wet and dry rot, and there were cockroaches everywhere. She carried out a campaign to get these people rehoused in new flats, but in doing that there came another problem.

In these houses it is easier to get to know your neighbours.

66 *In the old houses, they used to sit out on the corners and talk to one another. But when I visited them in the high-rise flats, things were so difficult. I went through a time of difficulties with those families – for they didn't see anybody, or have people to talk to.* 99

To meet the needs, she started organising theatre trips and other outings. It was a means of getting those people out of their homes and meeting one another. She had to beg people to give theatre tickets and minibuses at reduced prices because there was little money to spare. She worked to get people feeling that they mattered and that they belonged to the community and to one another. Many of the things she did in the 1960s are now taken for granted, but in those days people were less aware of the problems of living in flats. She wanted to find a way of compensating those families for the changes that had come about because of where they lived.

66 *It was partly guilt on my side. I had a conscience, because I had got them rehoused. What could I do? I had to find a way of doing something for them, and that's how all this community work came about.* 99

Racial prejudice

> **66** *When I came here thirty years ago I didn't know why people were acting as they were. I didn't know the word 'racism'. I had no label for them. All I could have said was that the white people were 'ungodly'. That was my view of them then. Only later did I see it as racism.* **99**

> **66** *When you've just come out of church and people cross the road and are waiting for the bus, and you cross over the road, get on the bus and say 'Bye' to them, and they just turn away. That was a real shock.* **99**

When she first came to Britain, Sybil Phoenix was confused by the way in which some people treated her. She had never before come across people who took a dislike to someone just because of the colour of his or her skin. To start with, she thought that she might have done something wrong to offend the. Then she assumed that they were simply being unpleasant to everyone. Only gradually did she come to understand that people could be prejudiced against people of another race.

What shocked her most at that time was that prejudice of this sort was also found among those who claimed to be Christian.

It was therefore a double shock for her – to find racial prejudice not just in society, but also in the Church. She was also bewildered to find that the way religious people behaved in Britain was different from what she had known in Guyana. She remembers seeing a vicar with his robes on, but with a cigarette in his mouth and a glass of whisky in his hand. That sort of thing would not have been seen in public in Guyana!

But what hurt most were the little things that people did not do or say to her, just because of her colour.

Until the Race Relations Act made it illegal for a person to discriminate against someone just because of their race, it was common to find people advertising rooms to rent and saying 'Whites only'. For those who had come to Britain in response to advertisements, and who thought that they were needed here and therefore that they would be welcomed, it came as a terrible hurt.

Sybil Phoenix has always feared that – because of the years in which they have been the victims of racial prejudice – black people may grow to feel bitter towards all white people. She believes that this could lead to a situation where black people cannot any longer accept the friendship of white people, even if that friendship is offered in good faith.

She feels that many of the problems with some young black people today come from the way in which they saw their parents being treated, at the time when there was very obvious racial prejudice. It is not something that they can easily forget. It may make them defensive, not wanting to trust white people, for fear that they too will be hurt.

Sybil Phoenix believes that it is a tragedy that young

> **"** It's little things that one would think don't matter that make life worth living. Sometimes I went home thinking 'I wonder what's the matter with me that she behaved like that towards me? What have I done?' And all the rest of the day it troubles you. **"**

> **"** It's different for young black people now, because they are not expecting what we were expecting. **"**

> **"** Black people came to this country loving, and white people rejected us. The days will come when they will want us to love them, but we will have been so hurt that we're not going to want them, we're not going to want their love. **"**

black people have grown up in an intolerant society that has not accepted them or given them equal status with white people. She sees herself trying to bridge the gap between the two cultures, so that they can understand one another better.

The way in which racial prejudice is shown may have changed since the 1950s, and Sybil Phoenix remains optimistic about the future, but there are new problems with young people from West Indian families who have been born in this country.

I want to do the same as everyone else!

I never behaved like that when I was a boy. My folks were strict with me.

But that was in the West Indies, Dad. People are different here!

Some parents, especially if they were brought up in a religious and strictly moral way, find it difficult to turn a blind eye, or accept that their children want to behave differently. Some young black people therefore feel that they are caught between two different groups – on the one hand, their parents do not understand them, but on the other, they may feel rejected by a white society.

An important part of the work of Sybil Phoenix with young people has been helping those of different races to understand one another, and to value one another as individuals, no matter what the colour of a person's skin.

19

Girls in care

Sybil Phoenix runs Marsha Phoenix House, where she is the 'house mother'. This is an eighteen-bed house which acts as a place of security for girls who, for one reason or another, have been excluded from their own homes. It was named after her own daughter, Marcia, who died in an accident.

Girls who are in need of care and protection are referred to her mainly by the social services. Some of them only stay overnight, but others are with her for two or three years. While they are at Marcia Phoenix House, they are helped to become independent and self-sufficient, and they may stay with her until they reach the age of seventeen and a half or eighteen. Some of them go on to college, and the house keeps a bed for them, so that they can return at the end of each term.

Part of her work with the girls is trying to get them together with their parents, so that they can talk through the problems which led to their being taken into care. Often, she organises counselling sessions where parents, daughters and social workers can all get together and discuss what is needed. Sometimes there are strong feelings about what went wrong in family life, and it is easy for people to blame one another, or feel guilty about what they have done. People may find that it is easier to cope with their feelings once they can talk about them.

❝ *Parents sometimes feel guilty; children may feel very bitter.* **❞**

❝ *No individual can exist as an individual. You can only use electricity, gas and water – things we take for granted – because many other people work together to make it possible. We therefore have a responsibility towards all those people who work for us. That is what society is all about.* **❞**

Living with an open door

Sybil Phoenix believes that you should have an open door, to welcome people, rather than being closed and locked away for fear that people will come and steal from you. If a thief is determined to come and steal, then there is little you can do to prevent it. The danger is that your fear of being robbed also stops you welcoming other people as well, so you lose out on their friendship.

An open door is also an attitude of mind. Sybil Phoenix welcomes and listens to many people. She tries to understand them, and shares her views with them. This leads other people to trust her, and to want her to speak on their behalf. It also enables her to bring together different people, and help them to listen to one another. By being

Sybil Phoenix has been awarded the MBE (Member of the British Empire medal) by the Queen for her work. She sometimes feels that young people themselves should be sitting on the various committees where she finds herself representing their needs – but for now, she continues to speak for them as 'Big Youth'!

open to them, she tries to help them be open to others.

Young people may come up against all sorts of problems – because of their race, because of where they live, because their parents do not understand them – and Sybil Phoenix has been involved with all of these.

Over to you

1 People in a neighbourhood cannot easily get to know one another unless they work together or share in some common activity or social event.
   ● Make a list of the clubs and societies in your own area. Do you know how many people attend them?
   ● Are there any other activities or organisations that you think would benefit people in your area? Give reasons for your suggestions.
   ● Do you think the area in which you live is a friendly one? If so, say how this friendliness shows itself. If not, say why you think it isn't.
   ● It may be useful to compare your answers with those of someone else who lives nearby.

2 In Britain there are race relations laws which aim to stop people from being victimised because of the colour of their skin.
   ● Although they may be necessary to protect people, do you think that laws can actually improve the way in which people of different races treat one another? What else is needed?
   ● List those things that you would expect to know about somebody before you would call him or her a good friend. Which (if any) of these depend on the race from which that person comes?

3 Sybil Phoenix has described a person who does not know about the country from which he or she has come as being like a tree without roots.
   ● Describe in your own words what you think this means.
   ● How do you think people who have moved from one part of the world to another can best stay aware of their roots? How may this affect the way in which they treat the society in which they have come to live?

Address for further information:

Marsha Phoenix House
90/92 Tressilian Road,
Brockley
London   SE4 1YD

Jonathon Porritt
CARING FOR THE ENVIRONMENT

Why should we be concerned about the state of the environment? What can ordinary people do to make this a cleaner, healthier and safer world? Is it possible to escape the consequences of the human exploitation and destruction of the natural world around us?

Jonathon Porritt left a career in teaching to become the Director of Friends of the Earth, an organisation that seeks to make people aware of the threats to the environment, and to help them to join together and do something to improve it. He now broadcasts and writes on environmental issues.

Born in 1950, Jonathon Porritt went to school at Eton, and then on to Oxford University, where he read Modern Languages. At that time he had no wish to be involved in politics, nor was he particularly concerned about the state of the environment. From an early age he had read the newspapers, and had taken an interest in political and current affairs, but he had never become actively involved in them.

Then he became a teacher. He worked in a London school for nine years, teaching English and Drama. He enjoyed this enormously, and assumed that he would carry on in education as his career. He only became Director of Friends of the Earth because of a chance set of circumstances coming together.

While teaching, he started to become involved in issues to do with the environment, and joined environmental organisations, like Friends of the Earth and Greenpeace. But he was still more a detached supporter than an active helper. At that stage he began to read a lot about the state of the Earth, and to think about the importance of 'green' issues, and from then on he found that he couldn't turn back from becoming 'greener' in his views.

> **"** *My own interpretation of why the world is in such a state is a very simple one: we have lost the capacity to revere God's Earth.* **"**

> **"** *I hadn't actually intended, or thought it was possible, to get a job in the Green Movement! I thought it was something that had to be done at weekends, in the evenings and in school holidays.* **"**

He started to be involved with politics, and became a member of the Green Party. In 1979 and 1983 he stood as a candidate at the general election, and he also stood in the elections for the European Assembly in Strasbourg in 1979 and 1984. From reading about the issues and being concerned, he had become an active campaigner – but all this was done in his spare time, while he continued to work as a teacher.

Then, in 1984, after nine years at the same school, he thought it was time for a change, and started looking for jobs. He was aiming to become a deputy headmaster somewhere, but – because of his part-time involvement – he was then invited to become Director of Friends of the Earth, working full time to help people care for the world in which they live.

Humankind and the Earth

Jonathon Porritt stresses that people need to have correct information about the state of the world. Once a person sees the world in a 'green' way, he or she may feel convinced that something **ought** to be done about it. There are practical problems which need practical solutions. This is a basic moral feeling that leads people to take practical action to show their concern for the Earth. But Jonathon Porritt also has religious reasons for his concern.

> 66 *We have learned how to use the Earth and exploit it, manipulate it and turn it into man-made wealth. But we have lost the art of reverencing it as something of immense power and immense beauty and of spiritual significance in itself – and until we get that right, it doesn't matter how many people go 'green' in terms of becoming environmentalists, or how many people join green parties. Unless we get the values side of it right, the political side of it is not going to solve our problems.* 99

Friends of the Earth does not represent any particular religous group, so it does not generally present any religious basis for the work it carries out, but many people know Jonathon Porritt's views on this, and at public meetings he often finds enthusiasm for this spiritual side of the commitment to care for the Earth.

66 *Once you've seen the 'green' light, as it were, you can't turn it off, it doesn't go away. You may decide to change your commitment to it, or to play it a different way. But once seen, it is there as a permanent part of your way of thinking.* 99

The Earth – 'something of immense beauty'.

Friends of the Earth

66 *I see the Earth as a living system, and I derive as much spiritual fulfilment and enrichment from the Earth itself as I do from any abstract idea of Christianity. I see the Earth as God's creation, and I see the beauty and diversity of it as the clearest sign of his creative power – so I find the two things (Christianity and the Earth itself) are wedded to one another. They are not in any way separate or hard to combine.* 99

A local group protests about lead pollution in the atmosphere.

When Jonathon Porritt first started working there in 1984, Friends of the Earth had only eight people on its staff and no money, and it owed thousands of pounds which it had spent appealing against the building of a nuclear power station at Sizewell in Suffolk. But a lot has changed over the last five years, and in 1989 Friends of the Earth had a staff of about eighty and a budget of five to six million pounds a year.

He doesn't claim that such growth has come about because they have been brilliant organisers, but because Friends of the Earth has been able to speak out on a particular set of concerns that many people have had about the environment. It also offers a practical set of alternatives, so that people can actually do something to help. As an organisation, Friends of the Earth has helped to shape the climate of opinion, which has changed greatly, but it has also grown and been shaped by that change.

There is an old approach to charity and pressure-group work – the idea that 'we are the experts, you give us the money and you won't need to worry yourself about it again'. Friends of the Earth has never been like that. When it started, it was made up of local group activists – people who wanted to get out and do something active about their environment – who happened to think that having a central organisation might be useful.

That attitude is still there in the way in which they work. People who join Friends of the Earth don't just get a thank you for their donation – they get information about how to contact their local group. They may also be asked to write letters. One of the most effective ways of making your concerns known is to write to your Member of Parliament, to a government minister, or to some other influential person. Sometimes letters are needed to protest against what is being done to the environment, or they may be part of a campaign for some new action to be taken.

In other words, people who join Friends of the Earth are invited to become active campaigners for the environment. If they don't want to do this, Friends of the Earth doesn't pester them; it simply puts them on the list of people who sympathise with its work, and are prepared to contribute money, but who do not want to take any action themselves.

Caring for the environment may not give you a life in the open air; it involves a lot of routine hard work. Jonathon Porritt needn't have worried about the amount of paper work that he had as a teacher – he has even more now!

❝ We are not just in the business of protest; we are in the business of finding answers, which is much harder. ❞

There are two separate networks within Friends of the Earth. There are the national supporters – over 170,000 of them – and there are also the local group networks, with 280 groups throughout Britain. No one really knows how many people belong to these groups, because they organise themselves.

There is only about a 20 per cent overlap between the two networks. Some people join locally, but do not belong to the national Friends of the Earth; others join nationally, but do not become active locally.

Most of the enquiries that Friends of the Earth gets from young people come from those who are doing GCSEs. At that age, people often want to commit themselves to doing something about these important issues, and some of them go on to become members of the Earth Action Groups – specially organised by Friends of the Earth for young people of fourteen years and over.

Friends of the Earth is not limited to Britain; there are groups now in thirty-five different countries around the world. In elections, too, there is more support for the 'green' parties. In the European elections in June 1989, the Green Party in Britain polled about 15 per cent of the vote. The 'green' vote is increasing all over Europe, and there are a group of 'Green' Members of Parliament now sitting in the parliament building in Strasbourg.

Some of the issues

The 'greenhouse effect'

Because of the way in which humankind is burning fossil fuel and releasing large amounts of carbon dioxide and other gases, a layer of these gases is building up in the upper atmosphere, which will act like the glass of a greenhouse – trapping the heat and gradually warming up the surface of the Earth.

The ozone layer

This is a layer in the atmosphere which protects us, and all forms of life, from the more harmful rays of the sun. Certain gases, especially the CFCs used in some aerosols and in the cooling system of fridges, are destroying this protective layer. As we release them into the atmosphere, so we increase the amount of harmful radiation that reaches the Earth.

Rubbish – we produce far too much of it!

Saving power

When you buy electrical goods, you should remember that some use less power than others. If people saved energy, there would be less need for more power stations – whether these are nuclear ones, with the danger of accidents (as at the Russian nuclear plant at Chernobyl) and the problem of getting rid of nuclear waste, or those that burn up our reserves of fossil fuels, like coal, which may add to the 'greenhouse effect'.

Motor cars

As more people use lead-free petrol for their cars, one danger to health is cut out, but it is hoped that in future all cars will be fitted with catalytic converters, which will filter out 90 per cent of all harmful pollution from their exhausts.

The Amazon rainforest

The destruction of vast areas of rainforest in Brazil is a threat to everyone, because the burning of the forest releases huge amounts of carbon dioxide into the atmosphere, which may increase the 'greenhouse effect'. Forests are destroyed in order to make a quick profit from the land. There are also plans to build huge hydroelectric dams, which would drown large areas of forest and drive the native Indians off their land. In many of the poorest parts of the world, those who live in poverty are forced to clear forest in order to get land to grow their crops. Often this land is unsuitable for farming, and within a short time it becomes useless.

> 66 *Rainforest – you either cut it down and make a quick buck for a very short period of time; or you leave it standing and make a slightly smaller buck for ever.* 99

> 66 *At long last, people are beginning to see the connections between the ecological tragedy of the Amazon and the basic injustice of a world economic order primarily shaped by* us *– by our banks, by our trading policies, by our involvement in far too many aid and 'development' projects which do down the poor as comprehensively as they assault the Earth.* 99

Oxleas Wood – a matter of priorities

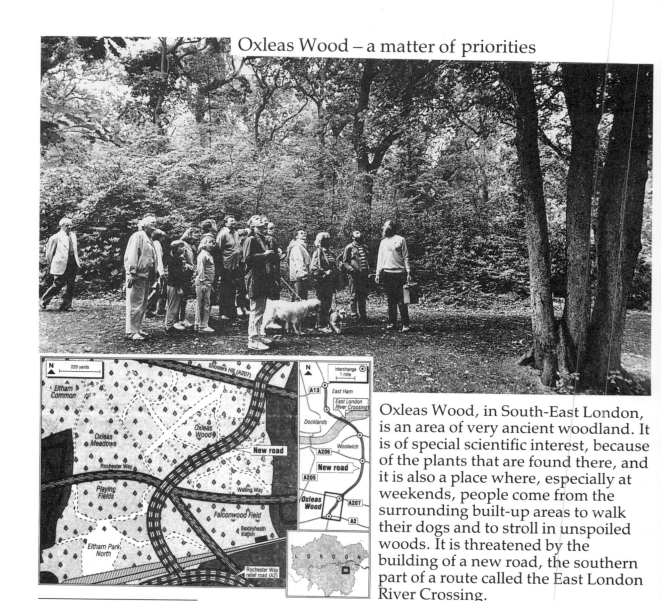

Oxleas Wood, in South-East London, is an area of very ancient woodland. It is of special scientific interest, because of the plants that are found there, and it is also a place where, especially at weekends, people come from the surrounding built-up areas to walk their dogs and to stroll in unspoiled woods. It is threatened by the building of a new road, the southern part of a route called the East London River Crossing.

> ❝ Oxleas illustrates the problems that a local community faces when it is up against a national momentum. The Department of Transport say that we have got to have more roads. ❞

When a new road is built, there is a planning inquiry, and this is an opportunity for groups like Friends of the Earth to make their views known. At Oxleas Wood, it had been suggested that a tunnel should be cut out, and then the trees replanted over the top of it. This would have added £15 million to the total cost of £200 million for the new road, and so this idea was rejected. Jonathon Porritt thinks that the Department of Transport should dig a proper tunnel under the wood, so that it is left undisturbed, and that the extra cost would be worthwhile.

Jonathon Porritt thinks that more people should become involved with the campaign to save Oxleas Wood.

66 *I'm amazed at the way in which some people manage to separate out their environmental concerns in such a way that they don't need to do anything. I mean, people get worked up about Brazil and enthusiastic about sending money there, but here is a piece of immensely ancient and important woodland near the middle of London, and there doesn't seem to be the same sense of outrage and urgency. I personally think that, if they decide to go ahead with that proposal, then we at Friends of the Earth will be calling on people to show the same kind of commitment that we expect the people in Brazil to show. We are very supportive of the rubber tappers and the Indian people who have organised blockades in their forest – and there may come a time when we will need to do the same thing here.* **99**

Do we really need more roads? If so, how much should we be prepared to pay so that they do as little damage as possible to the environment? How do you decide how much a piece of woodland is worth to those who enjoy it? Caring for the environment costs money, and people need to be persuaded that it is worthwhile. As with many such problems, it is a matter of priorities – which is more important for you, having new roads or saving the woodland?

Local people in Greenwich don't want to see their wood destroyed, and in a demonstration in 1988, two thousand of them went to the wood to lie down in front of a giant painting of a bulldozer, and to 'hug' trees, as a gesture of their support for them.

He believes that the same principles apply, whether you look at Oxleas Wood or the great rainforests. There are certain parts of our natural world that should be preserved, because of their importance to local people, the value of their plant and animal life, and the need to conserve them for the good of everyone. There are other parts of the natural world which, because of the needs of the human species, can't be preserved in this way. Yet we still ought to manage them as responsibly as possible.

Jonathon Porritt points out that there is a connection between our treatment of the Earth, and the way in which we want to develop and make money. Protecting the living Earth is also a matter of seeking justice for the people whose lives depend upon it – and that means all of us.

29

WHAT YOU CAN DO:

There are many ways in which you can help to prevent water pollution.

- Cut your energy consumption, and so your contribution to acid rain and the nuclear industry. Ask about energy efficiency when you buy any new electrical appliance.

- Buy organic food which has been grown without the use of chemical fertilisers and pesticides.

- Check the pipes in your house, and if they are lead, replace them. Ask your water company to replace any lead supply pipes.

- Report water pollution incidents when you see them to the National River Authority. FoE can advise you on how to do this.

- Recycle as much of your waste as possible, and so cut down the amount of waste that has to be dumped in landfills.

Water pollution

Industry often spills toxic chemicals; farmers use chemical fertilisers and pesticides on the land; factory farms produce liquid manure (called 'slurry'); waste is pumped into rivers from sewage works; acid rain falls over the land and seeps through into rivers and lakes. These are just some of the ways in which water is polluted – and Friends of the Earth has a Water Campaign, with practical ideas for preventing this sort of pollution taking place. People may ignore pollution when it affects other parts of the world, but water is something on which everyone depends for life. Typical of Friends of the Earth, their booklet on water pollution ends with a list of ways in which people can help.

While human beings pollute and exploit the Earth, other species suffer. This Guillemot, smothered with oil, lies dead on a beach in Dorset.

30

A glance through recent issues of the Friends of the Earth magazine, Earth Matters, *shows the wide range of things with which Jonathon Porritt and others are concerned. Some of the concerns are huge – like what should be done to protect the Antarctic from being exploited. Others concern the destruction of places of special scientific interest – where plants and animals are meant to be protected.*

Priorities

Of all the issues with which he is concerned, Jonathon Porritt thinks that the rainforests should come first. He argues that we won't sort out the problem of rainforests unless we find some solution to the debts that the poor countries owe to rich ones. And that means changing the unfair trade patterns, in which many tropical rainforest countries are not getting the proper value for the goods that they are exporting. And we won't solve that problem until we learn to develop and use the Earth's limited resources in a way that is reasonable, and which can be sustained without doing damage.

He believes that, if we can solve the problem of rainforests, we can get many other things right at the same time.

Address for further information:

The Education Officer
Friends of the Earth
26–28 Underwood Street
London   N1 7JQ

Other useful addresses:

Greenpeace
30–31 Islington Green
London   N1 8XE

The World Wide Fund for Nature
Panda House
Weyside Park
Godalming
Surrey   GU7 1XR

The National Trust
36 Queen Anne's Gate
London   SW1H 9AS

Over to you

1 Choose one or more of the issues with which Friends of the Earth is involved, and collect information on it. You may find articles in newspapers describing the problem, or news items about demonstrations organised by 'green' groups. Then try to draw up a list of the choices that people have to make if they are to solve the problems involved, and what action is needed.

2 Many people hope that, as each year passes, they will be able to improve their 'standard of living' – own more things, travel more quickly, use more energy in order to be comfortable.
   ● Do you think this attitude can be a threat to the environment? If so, why?
   ● In what other ways might you want to measure the quality of your life?

3 Our lives can be affected by things that are happening in many other parts of the world.
   ● Can you think of examples of this?
   ● What can you do to influence what happens in other countries?

4 Is there any place of natural beauty that you visit regularly? What part does it play in your life? How important is it to you?

Stuart Affleck

SHARING IN THE LIFE OF A CHRISTIAN COMMUNITY

Stuart Affleck is Warden of the community at Pilsdon Manor. Set in a beautiful part of the Dorset countryside, Pilsdon offers a place of love and acceptance for many people who have found life difficult, or who have been in some sort of trouble. It is a resting place for those who have no fixed home. It is also a Christian community, where a group of people live a life of prayer and practical work. Stuart Affleck has chosen to give up an income and privacy for himself and his family, in order to lead a way of life that offers little money and a constant stream of people wanting his help and advice, but which also gives him great freedom and satisfaction.

> 66 *People have wonderful resources in them. They just need a caring community – the right sort of environment in which to let their talents develop.* 99

Pilsdon Manor is an old house, set in open farmland about 6 miles from the sea. It is reached by narrow, twisting lanes, through a part of the Dorset countryside called the Marshwood Vale. Pilsdon itself is not really a village – there is just the manor house, a small church and a few scattered cottages and farms.

Here a community of people have chosen to live and work together. Some have made it their home, and live here permanently. They have chosen Pilsdon because it is a religious community, where they can share in Christian worship and live a simple, country life, caring for their many visitors. Others come to Pilsdon as guests, staying for a while, especially if they have been in some sort of trouble. Some have come from prison; some have no fixed place to live, but tramp the roads; some are trying to get used to living without alcohol or drugs; some just want a time away from the pressures of their usual life in order to think about what they are doing.

For Stuart Affleck, a Church of England clergyman, this is where he and his wife Judy have chosen to live and bring up their three sons. Stuart has been coming to Pilsdon since he was about fourteen years old. His parents used to take him on holiday to Charmouth on the Dorset coast, and one day they discovered Pilsdon, came to Evensong in the little church and in that way introduced him to the community.

At that age he thought that going to church in the ordinary way was boring, but to find a group of people who were actually trying to live out their religion really impressed him.

When I was fourteen, it all seemed a bit scary really, because I didn't know what to expect. It was all new.

How did it all start?

The community at Pilsdon Manor had been running for many years before the Afflecks arrived. It had become well known as a place to which people could turn if they were in trouble and needed time to think or recover from what had happened to them.

The community was started by Percy and Gaynor Smith in 1958. Important events in people's lives sometimes come from quite simple things, which seem to happen by chance, but which start a person thinking in a new way. It was rather like that with the idea of Pilsdon. In 1950 Gaynor Smith bought a book called *Nicholas Ferrar of Little Gidding*, to read on the journey back to Hong Kong, where the Smiths were living, after a holiday in England. It described the life and work of Nicholas Ferrar, who set up a community at Little Gidding in the seventeenth century. For many years he had lived in a community of Christians who had worked and prayed together, and who had welcomed all who wanted to visit them. Little Gidding had offered a place of peace, simple living and religion.

Although I don't think I ever really wanted to become a monk or anything like that, the idea of living in a community like Pilsdon attracted me.

It was reading this book that led Gaynor Smith, with her husband and daughter, to search for a place to found a community when eventually they returned to England. But it was several years before the opportunity came their way.

While Percy Smith was working as a clergyman in Devon, he heard that the little country church at Pilsdon in Dorset was to be closed because of lack of support. At about the same time, he heard that the manor house at Pilsdon was to be sold. These two things came together just at the right time. Once he and Gaynor saw Pilsdon, they knew that this was the place in which they could follow the tradition of Nicholas Ferrar, and set up their community.

They managed to buy the manor house, along with some land and a cottage. When they first moved in, they had little money, and nothing to make their life comfortable. To start with, local people and newspaper reporters wondered what a clergyman was doing trying to set up a community of this sort, but very soon those who lived at Pilsdon found that there was a need for a place like theirs. Although the community was a long way from main roads and towns, people started arriving there, asking to stay with them in order to take time away from the pressures of their lives.

> 66 *I never believed I'd live here, although I thought I might try to set up something like it in a town.* 99

How did Stuart come to be Warden?

Stuart Affleck was ordained as a priest in the Church of England. He worked in a parish and then as a school chaplain, but all the time he kept in touch with the community at Pilsdon. Although he was impressed with the idea of living in a Christian community, he thought that he couldn't simply repeat what the Smiths had done at Pilsdon. He thought that he might eventually try to set up a similar community elsewhere.

Then, when Percy Smith decided that it was time for him to retire, he suggested that Stuart might take over from him as Warden.

> 66 *It seemed a dream come true.* 99

The Affleck family arrived at Pilsdon in 1980. Stuart and Judy had three boys, aged two and a half, five and seven. They found that life at Pilsdon was very different from that of an ordinary clergyman. For one thing, they no longer had the privacy of being alone together as a family in a home of their own. They had to adjust to a new way of life, seeing how things developed and how best to organise their life together.

> 66 *You don't live in an ordinary house any more; you don't eat on your own. You share your space and your time with other people.* 99

As a priest, too, his life was rather different:

> 66 *Your congregation lives with you – so things you say in the sermon you have to live with through the following week. I have to live and work here, and some of my work does not seem to be very priestly – I have to take my share of ordinary jobs around the community.* 99

> 66 *I take my turn at mucking out the pigs – not what some people expect a priest to be doing!* 99

Stuart is on the right. Milking the cows is one of his favourite jobs.

"We all have to take a share in the work here – and it can get muddy!"

> 66 *It is based on a life of prayer and following the Gospels as close as we can. We pray four times a day.* 99

The main idea of the community is to provide a place where people can come and stay, sometimes for just a couple of days, sometimes for longer. They all live together and work together on the land. Everyone is accepted, no matter how troubled they are, or what reasons they have for wanting to come to the community.

Another important thing is that Pilsdon tries to be self-supporting, and those who stay there have to give a hand with all the jobs that need to be done around the house and fields. Although work like this is necessary, it is also a good opportunity for people to get to know one another, and feel that they are doing something useful for others.

As well as being a community who work together, Pilsdon is a place where people try to put the Christian religion into practice.

The eight people who live together as permanent members of the community have agreed to commit themselves to following Jesus Christ in that place at that time – in other words, while they are together, they agree to share a common religious life. This includes a routine of worship, which follows the tradition of the Anglican Church.

The religious life at Pilsdon was set up to follow a simple daily pattern. In some ways it is like a monastery, but community members at Pilsdon do not become monks or nuns, and they do not have to agree to stay there for the rest of their lives.

Combining work and prayer, the fixed daily routine is something that many people find helps them to discover peace and security in their lives, especially if they have been through a time of anxiety and change. This is the pattern of daily life at Pilsdon:

Matins and Holy Communion	7.30 a.m.
Breakfast	8.00 a.m.
Prayers	1.00 p.m.
Lunch	1.15 p.m.
Tea	4.30 p.m.
Evensong	6.30 p.m.
Supper	7.00 p.m.
Compline (evening prayers)	9.15 p.m.

66 *Our guests are welcome to come to services if they like, but they do not have to believe anything in order to stay here.* **99**

Who stays at Pilsdon?

66 *Love and unconditional acceptance is offered to everyone who comes.* 99

Stuart Affleck, his wife, six other adults and seven children form the permanent members of the community. They are not called 'staff', although they run the community, because they are not paid for the work they do. Instead, they live as members of the community, having food and other necessities provided for them. Everyone works for the benefit of the community, whether they are guests or permanent members, and everyone eats together.

There are, on average, twenty-two guests at any one time. Some of them may be students, who come from all parts of the world to stay for a while at Pilsdon. There may be children from inner cities, who have little chance to enjoy country life at home, staying for a while. Other people come to Pilsdon because they are in some sort of difficulty, or need to get away from the pressures of their life for a while.

66 *We don't advertise.* 99

Many of the guests who come to Pilsdon have fallen foul of society in some way. People may have been in prison, or may have become dependent on alcohol or drugs. Some of the guests have come because they had difficulty in coping with their personal relationships.

Some of the guests are referred to the Pilsdon community by doctors, probation officers or social workers. Others come because they have had the community recommended to them by others who have come and been helped by their stay.

Some of the guests may be desperately poor, others quite rich. It is not always a matter of money that makes a person happy or sad, but the kind of experience of life that he or she has had. Sometimes people who have all the comforts they could want find that their marriage breaks up, or they may feel anxious or confused about what they should do with their life.

66 *We tend not to put a limit of people staying. Some stay four or five years, others stay for only a few weeks.* 99

Pilsdon also provides food and a bed for the night for wayfarers, who tramp the roads with no permanent home. Sometimes they turn up on a Friday to get 'passing-through money'. This is a small allowance that the homeless can claim when they pass through a major town, but then they can't claim it from that place again for another week – so they pass on somewhere else. It's just a handout of four or five pounds. If they sign on for the money on a Friday, they can't get it until the next Tuesday.

66 *Many of them can't be bothered to wait around for it, so they move on.* 99

A stroll round Pilsdon

Stuart Affleck explains:

66 *The best way to show you Pilsdon is not by describing the few sensational people or dramatic situations we have had, because most people just quietly come into our lives and then quietly leave again. Let's just take a look around, and see what activities are going on here.* 99

"We have four cows – they produce enough milk for the community. We let the cream rise and then skim it off, to make our own cheese and butter."

"Although we grow all our own vegetables, we still have to buy an enormous amount of stuff."

66 *We have nine and a half acres altogether, with sheep, pigs, donkeys and hens. Some people who find it difficult to live with other human beings can relate to animals.* 99

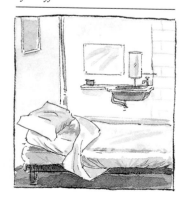

66 *Wayfarers just drop in; we have an average of about four a night. There is an increasing number of homeless people who are always on the move. We have our regulars, but many are unknown to us. Some professional wayfarers know how to live. The younger ones look for work, but find it difficult to get anything.* 99

"These all used to be animal boxes, and they have now been turned into human boxes. They get pretty cold in the winter, but people make themselves comfortable."

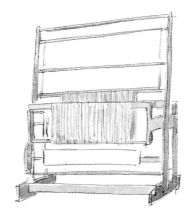

"People who find life difficult, because of the way our society works, find that, once they are here, no one is going to mind if they make a complete mess of what they are doing. That gives them the courage to try things they might have been afraid or embarrassed to do otherwise. We have an artist here who is starting to work again, after having been ill and unable to produce anything."

"We have services here, which are open to anyone. Because the community has been around in the Vale for more than thirty years, the locals generally accept us, even if they don't understand those who stay here. They are very kind, gentle and supportive. People come here for services from quite a wide area."

What does the Pilsdon community do

Those who stay as guests contribute something from what they have to live on. This is often money that they receive from the DSS (Department of Social Security) because they cannot find work. People staying at Pilsdon contribute most of their DSS money to the community, but keep the rest to spend on little personal needs – such as sweets, cigarettes and coffee. As a registered charity, Pilsdon can also receive gifts and legacies from those who want to support its work.

66 *I can get on and live without having to worry where the next penny is coming from. I feel very free.* **99**

Within the set pattern of daily life, people find themselves farming and gardening, cleaning the house or cooking the meals. All these things contribute to the life of the community. For some people, it is important to know that they are doing work which will help others – that they have something to offer, and that their contribution really matters.

But at Pilsdon, it is not just the work that people do that is important, but the atmosphere in which they share together. Members of the community are not concerned so much about what people have done in their life before they came, or why they needed to come – the most important thing is to accept the guests as they are, and then help them to relax and grow by sharing in their simple life and work.

In this way, work which could have been boring or depressing if done by a person who feels lonely or frustrated can become enjoyable because it is shared with others.

Pilsdon is not simply a place of rest for those who want to drop out of life, nor is it a kind of open hospital for those who have emotional troubles. It is a religious community, living the sort of life of sharing that its permanent members believe is the right way for Christians to live. They believe that people can be helped simply by going and sharing in that sort of community. Pilsdon can be rather like a family home, where people learn from one another, sometimes disagree with one another, but also learn about themselves by being together.

The community has little money. Its permanent members do not receive a salary, but they are given pocket money, and an allowance to enable them to go on holiday. Some who have money of their own actually manage to contribute to the cost of Pilsdon, as well as giving their time and their work. Do they feel cheated by not getting paid for the work they do? This is the answer Stuart Affleck gives:

66 *It's a matter of choice, and you have to make that choice for yourself. This is the way members of the community have always been. You live without a salary, but you live in a community that takes care of you. You don't have any bills to pay, and you have pocket money – about £40 per month.* **99**

> 66 *It would be nice sometimes just to get away and be alone.* 99

> 66 *I've always wanted to live this way.* 99

What is it like to be in charge of a community like this? Is there anything that Stuart Affleck misses from his former life?

> 66 *It wasn't difficult for me to come here to live, because I gave up one kind of life to do something that I'd always wanted to do anyway. The one thing you can't do, when you live in a community, is say on a Friday night 'That's it; I'm off with my friends', or something like that.* 99

Living together becomes quite tense at times, but in a community you can't escape; you have to stay and cope with the people around you.

Address for further information:

The Revd Stuart Affleck
Pilsdon Manor
Pilsdon-by-Bridport
Dorset   DT6 5NZ

Over to you

1 At Pilsdon there is a regular daily routine.
   - Do you have a routine for your own life? What do you do each day?
   - Do you think it is good to have a routine, or would you prefer every day to be different?
   - Why do you think most people who live in a community think that a routine of some sort is important?
   - Imagine that you are setting up a community. Devise a daily routine. What sort of rules would you want everyone to keep?

2 In what ways is the work that people do at Pilsdon different from just any ordinary job?

3 Do you think that Pilsdon is of most use to a person who is religious, or is it equally valuable for the non-religious person? List the sort of benefits you might expect from a stay in a community, and say whether or not you think these are religious.

4 Would you rather live in a community in the country or in a town? Give your reasons. How might the life at Pilsdon be different if it were in the middle of a big city?

5 List the advantages and the disadvantages of living in a community, rather than on your own or with your close family only.

Rowshon Malik

CAMPAIGNING ON BEHALF OF ASIAN WOMEN IN BRITAIN

Rowshon Malik works with groups of Asian women in Birmingham. She is an adult education co-ordinator, helping people to get the training courses they need. She also teaches them English, helps translate for them when they need to make themselves understood, and listens to their problems. As a campaigner for the rights of Asian women, she encourages them to continue their education and take up a career, if that is what they want to do.

Rowshon Malik is a devout Muslim, and leads discussion groups with other Muslim women about their religion – encouraging them to see that women have an important place in Islam. As a mother of four children, she knows the happiness of family life, but has also experienced the frustration of being at home, and the satisfaction of going back to work in order to use and develop her abilities.

> **66** *I want to help women build their self-confidence, get them out, educate them, so that they can help themselves. Women are just being used by society. They should feel that they are special and important.* **99**

Rowshon Malik came to Britain from Bangladesh in 1966. Her husband was already living in Britain, but went home to get married, bringing Rowshon back with him. She was a teenager and a student, and at first she felt depressed by the gloomy surroundings, after the sunshine of her homeland. Although she had freedom here, she felt that she was trapped in this country, and she was homesick. Even now, she misses her parents, who are still living in Bangladesh. This sadness at being separated from relatives affects many Asian women in Britain.

For many years, Rowshon Malik's life was devoted to bringing up her children, but then she felt that she needed to work outside the home, and eventually she became employed as a teacher of English as a Second Language.

She now works for the Adult Education Department. Half of her time is still spent teaching English to Asian

> **66** *My heart is always there, rather than here.* **99**

women, but she is also an adult education co-ordinator. This involves her arranging classes and groups, and also organising voluntary helpers. She also makes home visits, to find out the situation of the women who want to come to her classes, and to advise them.

Every week she meets about fifty or sixty women in her English classes. Almost every session, someone brings a message about a relative who has died or who is ill in Bangladesh, and then the women may start weeping, because they remember members of their own families who are so far away. Although it is important that these women should learn English in order to be able to improve their lives in British society, it is also important for them to meet to comfort and encourage one another.

Rowshon Malik leading a study group of Asian women.

66 *Sometimes I used to feel like a motherless child. Sometimes I used to feel like an eagle in the sky.* **99**

66 *I always give them some time to speak about their personal problems.* **99**

She is also the organiser and president of Dawalul Islam Women's Group, which meets for about an hour and a half on Saturdays. They discuss Islam, and the role of women in their religion. Sometimes Religious Studies students come to listen in on these groups, in order to understand more about what it is like to live as a Muslim.

Rowshon Malik is involved in the Bangladesh Women's Association, where she arranges religious activities. She is one of six trustees who worked for three years to set up the Muslim Women's Centre, in Mosely, which was opened in 1988. This is a training centre which caters especially for Muslim women who are very strict about their religious traditions and who would not feel comfortable using other facilities.

Language

Many Asian women have difficulty in finding the time to learn English. They are too busy in their homes, cooking, cleaning and looking after their children. They are often misunderstood when they go into hospitals, or speak to people from the social services. It is especially difficult for them to explain the problems they have with their teenage children. Without a good interpreter, such women are unlikely to get the help they need.

> 66 *I try to help women by taking them to clinics and interpreting for them.* 99

Muslims at school

Muslims are concerned to teach their children about Islam, and about the food, dress and customs of the Muslim way of life. When those children arrive at school, they will not find anything that goes directly against their religion, but there may be some practical difficulties. When they go to the toilet, there may be no water containers for washing themselves, which is required in Islam. At dinner time, they may be offered pork (which Muslims are not allowed to eat), and the food will not have been prepared in the traditional way. Even the fat used for frying chips may be animal fat, which is totally forbidden for Muslims.

For a Muslim child, problems may start here, in the school canteen.

Some children may not feel strongly about their religion, and may want to be like their friends at school. Then they find that they are going against the wishes of their parents, and this can lead to family arguments. Schools which have Asian pupils need to be aware of the special needs that they have.

Some Muslims argue that there should be more Muslim schools in Britain, where worship and religious education would be based on the teachings of Islam, and which would promote Muslim values – just as Catholic or Jewish schools promote the values of their religions. Mrs Malik's own children attended a Catholic school. She was happy with this because she believes that the Christian and Muslim religions share many beliefs and values, but she would have liked to have had the opportunity of sending them to a Muslim school.

Parents know that it is their duty to teach their children about Islam. Once they reach the age of sixteen or eighteen, it is up to them to decide whether or not to practice their religion, but until then the responsibility lies with the parents. In some ways, Rowshon Malik thinks that this is easier for Muslims in Britain because when you leave your own country you feel a bit homesick, and religion is one way of keeping in touch with the traditions of the land from which you have come. Practising their religion is one way in which Asian Muslims can feel that they belong to one another as a community.

Muslims will allow their children to go to mixed schools, but they prefer single-sex schools if possible. In some traditional Muslim communities, girls and boys of secondary school age are not encouraged to mix freely.

66 *People should have the right to choose for themselves what sort of school their children attend.* 99

Women in Islam

Rowshon Malik believes that women's place in Islam is completely misunderstood by people in the West:

66 *People think that Islam has made women a second-class race, without equal rights, powers and respects. That's quite wrong! According to Allah, women are very special; without women nothing would be fulfilled, because Allah made them gentle, kind and flexible.* 99

66 *Men and women are equal before Allah, although they have different roles.* 99

If a Muslim girl is intelligent, she should have all the education and professional training possible.

Some people mix religion and culture together, and they get into a muddle.

Although they may be strict Muslims, Mrs Malik points out that Asian women are increasingly coming out to attend classes in English, and are taking part in other social activities permitted in Islam. There is nothing to stop them, as long as they remain within the guidelines set out in Islam.

Although there are some limitations on what Muslim women should do, these are designed not to hinder them, but to protect them. In particular, Islam insists that men have a responsibility towards the welfare of women. When a family inherits money, a woman is supposed to receive only half as much as her brother – but this is because Islam assumes that she will have a husband to provide for her, or (if she is not married) that her parents will look after her.

There is a saying of the Prophet Muhammad that a man came to him and asked, 'Who is the most deserving of good care from me?' He replied, 'Your mother.' He repeated this answer three times, and only then went on to say, 'Your father' and then 'Your other relatives'. There is another tradition that the Prophet said that the best men were those who were kindest to their wives.

Rowshon Malik points out that the search for knowledge is compulsory for every Muslim, male or female. This goes against the popular idea that Muslim women are not allowed to go out or seek higher education. This misconception has come about because some Muslims are very protective of their daughters. It is a rule that, before a Muslim woman goes out and appears in public, she should cover her body and wear loose clothing, so that her figure will not show. She should also lower her eyes when she meets strangers. This is because Islam insists that women should behave in a modest way, and it aims to prevent a woman from attracting men to fall for her.

Even some Muslims have the wrong idea about this – especially those who are from remote areas. The trouble is that many people were taught to recite the Qur'an (the Muslim holy book) in Arabic, but they were not taught the translation, and therefore they did not understand its meaning. They follow the traditions of the culture from which they come, and make the mistake of thinking that the rules come from their religion.

Rowshon Malik thinks that Islam is not a difficult religion to understand. Allah promised that Islam is a straight path – if someone follows it, he or she sees clearly what should be done. The problem is that people confuse their religion with the traditions that they may have inherited from their parents. She meets with people every day who don't let their daughters go out, and who think that this makes them good Muslims, but they have little knowledge of Islam. She argues that a Muslim girl should

66 *One day I went to a group and they asked me what I thought about Asian women and European women. Who did I think were better off? I said that I felt sorry for Western women. Think of all that they have to do; all their responsibilities. They work so hard – a full-time job, then looking after the children, coming home after work and starting the housework. They try to make it nice, to please their husbands. They do everything! I wouldn't have all that to do if I were living in Bangladesh. Asian women may not have such luxurious things, but they don't have the number of duties either!* **99**

Are Western women any more free than Asian women? Are Western fashions a sign of freedom, or of sexual exploitation? What image do you have of yourself?

be allowed to have a proper education, and develop her abilities. The important thing is that she should behave and dress modestly. Some parents are too frightened to take these risks with their daughters. They are over-protective.

Is society fair to women?

In the course of her work, Rowshon Malik finds that most Asian women have a low opinion of themselves, and they often feel depressed. This prevents them from taking advantage of the opportunities that are offered to them. So she spends some of her time just talking to them and encouraging them to stand up, look around, get out of the house and do something! She argues that the Muslim religion does not hinder them from getting more out of life; it should make them feel special.

She is also critical of the place of women in Western society. They may think that they are so free, and that they have everything they want, but when she arrived in Britain as a teenager she looked at the women around her and thought, "These poor women, they are being used like commodities in TV adverts. Men are just using them. I would not want to accept that!"

Marriage

In Islam, it is expected that a woman will marry and bring up a family. A Muslim wife has a duty to look after her children and to keep house, and she should be in charge of everything in the home.

The Qur'an says that a man should provide for his wife and children, and he promises to do this when he marries. But if a man cannot manage to do this, then his wife can help him by working outside the home. Because marriage is a partnership, the wife should be prepared to work, if they need more money.

Rowshon Malik feels strongly that a woman should also be able to take up a career if she wants to do so. The main thing is that she should make sure that her home and family do not suffer because of it, and she should accept that it is her husband who has the responsibility for providing for the family.

Muslim women have always had control over their own money. When she marries, a bride should be given a dowry by the bridegroom, and whatever money she has or earns belongs to her. Her husband is not allowed to use it without her permission, and she can spend it or give it away in any way she likes.

In a traditional Muslim country, a wife returns to her family if she and her husband divorce. In the Asian sub-continent, divorced women may suffer badly because of this. Their family will take them in, and try to look after them, but they may already be desperately poor. In Britain it is easier because there is help provided by the government for single-parent families, and women are able to claim this.

Rowshon Malik knows many women through her groups who are either divorced or widowed. Often they struggle to keep house for four or five children. She has suggested to some of them that they should remarry, for this is encouraged in Islam. But some of them reject this idea. They prefer to cope single handed because they are afraid that their children may suffer from having a new man in the family. This is an important thing about Muslim women – they are generally prepared to sacrifice their personal lives for the sake of their children.

In Islam, parents who have a daughter are responsible for the way in which she behaves while she lives at home

I want to go out to work.

Why? What's the point? We have enough money; you can stay at home.

But I want to do something useful!

Do it then, but keep your money to yourself! I'm the one who should provide for this household.

I get the money and the satisfaction – and he keeps his self-respect.

66 *I suggested to them that they should remarry. My husband and I would have found suitable men for them, but they didn't want to. Their children had to come first.* **99**

> **That is why daughters are very special, and they are with us for a very short while. Once they are married, we cannot demand anything from them.**

> **I think that women are not having their fair share.**

> **I'm all for women!**

with them, and they should make sure that she marries someone suitable. Once she is married, she will go to live with her husband's family, and her parents' responsibility for her is diminished.

With a son, the situation is rather different. Sons marry and bring their wives home.

Although Rowshon Malik works to encourage Muslim Asian women to stand up and take a pride in themselves, to develop their abilities and to understand their own religion, she is also a campaigner for women of all cultures, and belongs to the Multi-faith Group in Birmingham. Being a devout Muslim, she is modest and quietly spoken, but she is radical and determined in her campaign to help Asian women in Britain.

Over to you

1 List the advantages and disadvantages of the Muslim attitude towards family finance and responsibilities, compared with those commonly found in the West.
- Which system do you prefer?
- Imagine that you are a Muslim woman wanting to go out to work. Write down, or act out, the discussion that you might have with your husband – giving his arguments against you working, from a traditional Muslim position.

2 Look back at the two sketches of typical forms of women's dress – Western and Asian. What does each of them tell you about the person who wears it? (List the things that come into your mind as you look at each of them.)

3 In the eyes of some Western people, Asian Muslims may be over-protective towards their daughters, limiting their social and working life.
- What rules do you think it is right for parents to lay down about the way in which their children behave and dress? (Say at what age these rules should start to apply, and when they should stop.)
- Do you think the rules should be different for girls and boys?
- Do your answers to this question put girls at an advantage or a disadvantage socially, compared with boys?

Jimmy Savile

HAVING FUN, HELPING PEOPLE AND RAISING MONEY FOR CHARITIES

Jimmy Savile is a disc jockey and a radio and television presenter, and he raises large sums of money for charity. He combines a genuine concern for those in need with a mischievous sense of humour, and a flare for wearing and doing the most outrageous things.

For many years he has also worked as a voluntary helper in hospitals, first of all at Leeds Infirmary, but also at Broadmoor and Stoke Mandeville hospitals. He is a Catholic, but is constantly involved with many other religions. The attitude he takes towards people reflects the Christian values of forgiveness and love. He also has a direct, no-nonsense way of sorting out people's problems and getting something done about them.

Jimmy Savile was born in 1926 in Leeds, Yorkshire, and was the youngest in a family of seven children. At the age of eleven, although he was too young to be employed, he used to play the drums for a local dance hall band after school. For this he was given ten shillings a week (50p). For a boy of his age, in those days, that was a lot of money! Although he was small for his age, and came from a poor family, he was able to mix with people from all walks of life, enjoy himself, and also get paid.

He left school at fourteen, and worked for a year in an office. It was wartime and he wanted to join the Air Force, but his eyesight was not good enough. Those who could not fight still had to help the war effort, and he was told to work in a coalmine. It was a very hard life, and he had to get up at half past four every morning, but he kept it up for seven years.

At first he worked at sorting coal above ground, but the machines were very noisy and he was covered with coal

66 *Money and fame may be fun, but they aren't everything.* **99**

Jimmy Savile reckons that a sense of humour helps.

66 *Laughing at ourselves is a great tonic.* **99**

dust all the time. Then he chose an unpopular job underground. It was dark and quiet, and he was left for hours on his own, which would have driven some people mad. But it gave him plenty of time to read, which he did by the light of his miner's lamp. His reading made up for what he had not learned at school.

He had an accident in which he hurt his back, and this forced him to leave the mine. He started working as a dance hall manager, eventually running the very dance hall in which he had played the drums as a boy. Jimmy Savile became a well-known, popular character, especially since he took to dying his hair different colours! Then he did something which was to be the start of his new career. Earlier, he had set up a gramophone for a birthday party, and had earned himself £2.50 for an evening's work playing and introducing records. He decided to try the same thing in the dance hall he was running – playing records for people to dance to, instead of having a band. This was a great success – he had become a disc jockey!

Jimmy Savile was invited to do a show for Radio Luxembourg. He managed to fit it into his day off from managing the dance hall, but he very quickly found that he could earn more money on that day than during the rest of his week.

When Top of the Pops *started in 1964, he presented the first programme, and from then on his face became well known all over the country. Previously, in radio, his name and his voice were known, but he could still go around in public without being recognised. Now he was a celebrity, who could cause a sensation wherever he went. From the hard life in the mine, with little money, he found himself with money and fame – and all this by doing what he enjoyed!*

Jimmy Savile at Radio Luxembourg in 1967

66 *My new world was a complete fairy tale, and it still is.* **99**

Jimmy Savile is always a familiar face in the television coverage of the London Marathon – an event through which he raises large sums of money for charity.

A life of success, with more money than you need – some people might call that perfect. But is it enough? Jimmy Savile was very happy with his life, but being famous brought with it problems, and he liked to keep in touch with ordinary people, sharing with them their own hopes and their sorrows.

Life in the pop world is not easy. For three weeks he worked as compere for the Beatles, and saw the wild enthusiasm of their young fans. He also saw how tough the pop world could be – one minute a person could be heading for stardom, and the next he or she could be out of fashion and ignored. Pop musicians have come and gone, but Jimmy Savile remains popular with people of all ages and from all walks of life. As a disc jockey on the commercial radio, his voice has become familiar everywhere.

Beyond the world of pop

One of the reasons for his continuing popularity is that, through his radio and television programmes and through charity events, Jimmy Savile is known to millions of people who might not listen to pop music. One of his early programmes was called *Speakeasy*. This was a chat show, organised by the BBC Religious Department. On it, Jimmy Savile interviewed many Church leaders, politicians and other influential people, in front of a studio audience.

Probably the best known of all his television shows is *Jim'll Fix It*, in which he tries to make the dreams of young people come true, by arranging for them to do something that they've always wanted. On that programme, Jimmy Savile shows what young people are capable of doing, given the chance, and also the tremendous amount of good will among those who help arrange the things that he has 'fixed'.

Keeping fit and alert

Jimmy Savile has always been determined to keep himself healthy. Even early on in his career, after a long evening's work in a dance hall, he would set out after midnight and go running for several miles. He still keeps himself very fit, and is a keen marathon runner.

He also enjoys walking, and once walked from John O'Groats to Lands End – the whole length of Britain, a total of 937 miles. The walk took him four weeks, and he arrived at Land's End to be greeted by great crowds of people and the band of the Royal Marines playing 'Congratulations'. He reckons he signed twenty thousand autographs along the way!

Jimmy Savile doesn't gamble and doesn't drink. He has seen the lives of many people in the pop world ruined by drink or drugs, and has always been determined that it would not happen to him. He feels that it is important for people to take charge of their own lives, and they can't do that when they are drunk. He shows that it is quite possible to stay fit, sober and alert, and still to have great fun at the same time.

Working for charity

66 *How about me as a porter, two days a week for a month?* **99**

Jimmy Savile has made a great deal of money, and is a good businessman, but he thinks that money is of little use unless it is set to work to help people. Although he earns about £250,000 a year, he raises much more than this for all sorts of charities.

But it is not just a matter of giving money. He wanted to do something practical to help people, and liked to keep in touch with ordinary folk, not just those who appeared on television and radio. He went along to his local hospital – Leeds Infirmary – and offered his services.

He found that working as a porter was a marvellous job. It brought him into touch with all sorts of people who were ill, and it started to become almost another way of life for him. He found that it gave him time to think about, and face up to, the deep things of life.

Today, Jimmy Savile spends about 90 per cent of his time doing charity work, and the remaining 10 per cent is occupied with earning money. He can manage to do this because he is paid so well for his broadcasting, but he has chosen to limit the amount of money-making work that he

> **“** *After the novelty of having lots of money wears off, it becomes relatively unimportant. Therefore, having reasonably provided for my old age means lots of money-earning capacity but not so much need, so what better than to make it for someone else.* **”**

is prepared to do. This is because he wants to be able to lead a very different kind of life. Many people who earn a lot of money might simply want to earn more – Jimmy Savile has decided that there are more important things to be doing.

Often it is because Jimmy Savile has decided to take part in an event that other people start to support it and give their money. In this way, even without giving the money himself, he is able to raise very large sums for all sorts of projects.

Just because charities help people when they are in need, it doesn't mean that those who do charity work have to remain serious. Those who have seen Jimmy Savile on television will know that he is always full of fun, and ready to play all sorts of tricks. His sense of fun is infectious – he has a way of getting other people involved in it.

The National Spinal Injuries Centre

Jimmy Savile has worked at Stoke Mandeville Hospital for many years, as a voluntary helper. He was already well known at the hospital when disaster struck the National Spinal Injuries Centre – an internationally famous centre for treating people who have been paralysed by accidents – which is based there.

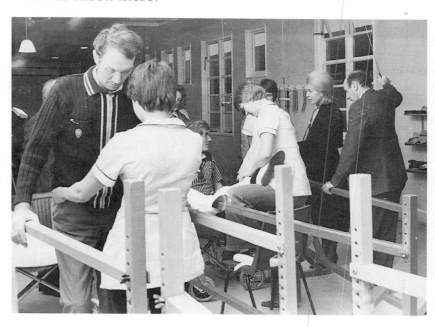

Patients and staff at the National Spinal Injuries Centre, during a visit by Her Royal Highness the Duchess of Kent.

> *Next morning I woke up with a £10 million headache!*

In August 1983 the specially designed new buildings of the National Spinal Injuries Centre were opened by the Prince of Wales. On the roof, coloured tiles spell out the word 'WELCOME', to greet patients who are flown in by helicopter.

A triumphant Jimmy Savile outside the new building.

> *Thanks to this marvellous new centre, these people are going to have hope, and they are going to have help, and the finest facilities, and they are going to have the dignity so necessary for a human being who is laid low. That's what it is all about, to give dignity back to the people who come here.*

The centre had been housed in old wooden huts. During the bad weather of the winter of 1979, the ceilings started to collapse, water flooded in, and patients were moved to other parts of the hospital. It was not practical to repair the old huts, but a new building would be very expensive. What should they do? To abandon the idea of a Spinal Injuries Centre would mean that patients would have to be treated in general hospitals, without the special knowledge that was available at Stoke Mandeville. A group of former patients chained themselves to beds in the derelict wards in protest.

Jimmy Savile approached members of the government, and received permission to launch an appeal for £10 million to rebuild the centre. Over the next few years, people responded by holding fund-raising events all over the country.

The whole appeal was organised by Jimmy Savile and a team of volunteers – with the result that all the money raised could go into the buildings, rather than being wasted in fund-raising expenses.

The majority of patients at the Spinal Injuries Centre are young people who have been injured in accidents. Injuries to the spine often leave people paralysed, and each patient at the centre is given a special routine of treatment to help him or her to regain as much movement as possible, and to strengthen the muscles that are still working. It is a place of great courage. A young person may be fit and well one minute, and then, suddenly – because of a road accident, or falling off a horse, or an injury on the sports field – he or she is flown to Stoke Mandeville, and may have to face the prospect of a life confined to a wheelchair.

Broadmoor Hospital

Broadmoor is a top-security hospital for those who are mentally ill, and who have a tendency to be dangerous or violent. Some of the five hundred patients have committed serious crimes, like murder. About three-quarters of them have severe personality disorders, and they are kept in Broadmoor because they could be a danger to themselves or to other people if they were allowed out.

Some patients respond well to treatment, and are able to leave Broadmoor. In 1988, for example, forty-four patients left the hospital – to go either to other hospitals which deal with mental illness, or to community hostels.

Jimmy Savile has been honorary entertainments officer at Broadmoor for more than twenty years. He gives his time to help the patients, and all the staff know to call on Jim at any time for his own brand of help and advice.

In 1988 he was put in charge of reorganising the way Broadmoor Hospital is run. He wants to see more help given to individual patients, so that they can be cured and go back into the normal world outside the hospital, without danger of any harm being done. Some of the patients have been there for a very long time, and would not know how to cope with life outside the walls. It is very difficult to help people like that – they need to be made to feel that they matter, and be helped to do things for themselves, so that they will not always be so dependent on other people.

> 66 *The staff are experts at helping and their high training standards mean high curing ratios.* 99

Jimmy Savile has been given many awards, including an honorary Law degree from Leeds University. He is a Catholic, and has received awards and medals from the Church, in recognition of his work. He was given the OBE (Order of the British Empire medal) in 1971, for his voluntary work, and in 1990 he was made a Knight of the British Empire-so his official title is 'Sir James!'

In 1989 it was estimated that Jimmy Savile had raised altogether £30 million for charities. Although he enjoys the things that money can provide – nice cars, holidays, different places to live – he still thinks that the most important things for him are the simplest. More than anything else, he enjoys running alone in the Yorkshire Dales.

Over to you

1 What are your ambitions? What work would you like to do, and how much money do you think you will earn doing it?
   - Are there jobs that appeal to you, but would not earn you as much money as you might get elsewhere? Would you seriously consider them as a career?
   - If you had more money than you needed, what would you do? Would you carry on working to earn still more? Would you consider doing voluntary work? Give your reasons.

2 Those who do voluntary work often say that they get great satisfaction from it. List those things that you believe can make work satisfying, other than the money that it can earn for you.

3 People who live in a hospital (like Broadmoor Hospital) sometimes become dependent upon it, and would not know how to cope with life in the world outside.
   - In what ways do you think the staff in places like that can help those who stay there feel that they still matter?
   - What are the main differences between living in an institution and living on your own? Why do you think people sometimes find it difficult to cope with the change when they leave?

4 If you had the chance to appear on *Jim'll Fix It*, what would you want Jimmy Savile to fix for you to do? Give reasons for your choice.

Handa Sage Shonin

WORKING FOR PEACE AS A BUDDHIST MONK

What difference have nuclear weapons made to the world? How can we find a sense of peace within ourselves? How can we promote peace? These are questions asked by Handa Sage Shonin, a Buddhist monk living in Milton Keynes. He has chosen to give his life to the discovery of inner peace, through the Buddhist religion, and to promoting peace and friendship between people of all nations and religions. He explains why he felt dissatisfied with his life in Japan, how he became a monk, and why he is committed to working for peace and opposing nuclear weapons.

> 66 *By building peace pagodas, we express Buddha's teaching that we should not kill, but that all people should have respect for one other.* 99

> 66 *I was just graduating from high school at eighteen years old, and I thought that, if I enter this society, and start to share its values, it will be difficult for me to get out of it again.* 99

As you approach the new city of Milton Keynes in Buckinghamshire, you may notice a circular building with a pointed roof, standing in open parkland. In front of it is a lake, and behind it, on the side of a low hill, are a thousand cedar and blossoming cherry trees. This is the peace pagoda, built in 1980 by a group of Japanese Buddhist monks and nuns. It expresses their hope for peace throughout the world, and is designed to give those who see it a sense of inner peace.

Handa Sage Shonin is one of those Buddhist monks ('Shonin' means monk, and it is a title added to his name). He was born in Japan. Although his mother was quite religious, he was not brought up to follow the Buddhist religion, and until he was sixteen years old, he had no particular plans about what he should do with his life. Then he started to think seriously about the society in which he lived. He looked at the problems people had in their lives, and the values by which they lived, and started to feel dissatisfied.

He saw that most people were too busy working and earning money. They had no time to stop and think about the meaning of life. Their only concern seemed to be that they should have a nice car, a good house, a stereo and all those sorts of things. Handa didn't like this attitude, and felt that there had to be something more to life than buying things to make you comfortable. As time went on, he became convinced that he had to look for something better.

In Japan, as in all countries, people enjoy shopping for luxury goods. But is this really what life is about? Handa was not convinced.

66 *Something moved me. I think I was trying to find myself; to discover who I really was. I was looking for something to which I could devote all my life.* 99

66 *I started to live there with Guruji and his disciples, and I helped with the building work. At that time, I knew that I had found what I was looking for, and that I would become a monk. In 1978, just before the opening ceremony for the peace pagoda in Sri Lanka, Guruji ordained sixteen young people, and I was one of them.* 99

Handa left Japan, and went to India. He didn't particularly know why he chose India as a place to visit, but he felt drawn to that country. He had no definite plans, but was just wandering around, looking for something to make sense of his life.

He came across a Japanese Buddhist temple in India, and met the monks who lived there. They told him that The Most Venerable Nichidatsu Fujii – founder of the Buddhist community of Nipponzan Myohoji – was going to spend some time in Sri Lanka. Since his visa to stay in India had almost expired, Handa decided to go to Sri Lanka to see him.

At that time, Guruji (which means 'respected teacher', and is the way in which the monks and nuns of Nipponzan Myohoji refer to the founder of their order) was working with his disciples and the Sri Lankan people to build a peace pagoda. This was on Sri Pada, a mountain which is thought of as a particularly holy place for Sri Lankan Buddhists.

Buddhism and peace

By becoming a monk, Handa has accepted special rules and traditions that do not apply to other Buddhists. He shaves his head as a sign of his dedication to the monastic life, wears the traditional saffron yellow robes of a monk, and has only the very minimum of personal possessions.

Most Buddhists are not monks or nuns. They live and work like everyone else, but try to put the Buddha's teachings into practice in their lives. They seek to live in a peaceful way, not harming any other creature, being generous, honest and restrained in their everday lives, and always having a clear mind – not dulled or confused by drink or drugs. All Buddhists, from all the different traditions of that religion, try to promote peace. The distinctive thing about Nipponzan Myohoji is that it was founded because of the horror of nuclear war, and it tries to promote international peace by supporting peace campaigns and by building peace pagodas.

Peace in a nuclear world

The city of Hiroshima – after the bomb.

On the morning of 6 August 1945, at the end of the Second World War, an American bomber flew over Hiroshima, in Japan, and dropped a single bomb. It did not hit the ground, but exploded 500 metres above the city, blasting the buildings below it and creating a great fireball. A few days later, a similar bomb was dropped on the city of Nagasaki. These are the only atomic bombs to have been used in war. Although they were small compared with modern nuclear weapons, they were several thousand times greater than any previous bombs.

Preparing for the first atomic test at Alamogordo, in the deserts of New Mexico. A bomb similar to this one was dropped on Hiroshima.

The sixth century CE was also a time when people built many pagodas and temples. The pagodas were to remind people of the Buddha's teaching, and therefore to encourage them to respect other people and to do them no harm. Nichidatsu Fujii decided that, in order to promote peace in a world threatened by nuclear weapons, he would build pagodas – not only in Japan, but throughout the world.

These small atomic bombs caused terrible destruction and killed about 140,000 people. Some of these died straight away as a result of the damage done by the explosion, but others died later because of various illnesses brought on by the radiation that nuclear weapons give out. It is this radiation, and the long-term damage that goes with it, which makes nuclear weapons so different from ordinary (conventional) ones.

With the coming of these atomic weapons, and the destruction they caused in his country, Nichidatsu Fujii (the founder of Nipponzan Myohoji) realised that, from now on, the whole idea of war had changed. This was total war: it involved everyone. Before the coming of nuclear weapons, it was possible for armies to fight one another – one side would win and the other would lose. Fujii saw that there can be no winner in the war fought with these nuclear weapons – both sides would be destroyed.

So Nichidatsu Fujii tried to think about what he could do to prevent the destruction of all people through nuclear weapons. He looked back at the history of Japan, and saw that when the Japanese government and people first accepted the Buddha's teaching (in the sixth century CE), there had been a time of peace. This happened because the very first precept (or principle) of Buddhism is that people should not kill one another, but treat each other with respect.

What is a pagoda?

A pagoda is a shrine built in honour of the Buddha, Siddharta Gautama, who lived in the sixth century BCE. Pagodas are simple and beautiful, and it is hoped that a person who stops to look at them will experience something of the peacefulness that Buddhism teaches. At the front of the peace pagoda at Milton Keynes there is an image of the Buddha, and around it are seven sculptures, showing scenes in the Buddha's life.

On the front of the pagoda is an inscription:

'May eternal peace prevail on Earth'

Buddhists believe that the only way in which peace is going to be possible on Earth is for each person to discover an inner peace. Some Buddhists describe this as the 'Buddha nature' that each person has within himself or herself. Most people, worrying about the problems of life, or thinking of what they want to achieve for themselves, do not recognise that they have this Buddha nature. By seeing the peace pagoda, people may be reminded that they can live in a peaceful way, just like the Buddha.

The pagoda at Milton Keynes was the first peace pagoda to be built by the Nipponzan Myohoji community in the Western hemisphere. It was opened in 1980 at a ceremony conducted by Nichidatsu Fujii himself. Today there are four ordained members of the order living at Milton Keynes, and another two at the second peace pagoda, built in Battersea Park in London.

66 Whether they are Buddhist or not – it doesn't matter – people come here and they think about peace. They may come and just sit and meditate. This is the presence of the Buddha here. 99

A demonstration or march may achieve two things. It may get publicity – perhaps appearing on television or radio – and therefore make other people think about.the need for peace. It may also be a means of bringing people together to encourage one another and to find out how much they have in common.

Working for peace

In campaigning for peace, and for a world free from the threat of nuclear weapons, Handa and other members of his community join in peace demonstrations and marches as much as possible. In 1979, members of Nipponzan Myohoji went on the 500-mile peace walk organised by CND (the Campaign for Nuclear Disarmament). This was soon after the opening of the peace pagoda, and it was a time when CND and other groups were not well

> 66 *We are not doing anything political when we campaign against nuclear weapons; we are just showing our religious beliefs. For Buddhists, not killing other creatures is the first precept, it is essential. There are other people on demonstrations – Christians, Communists or whatever – but we can all share this point of belief.* 99

Beneath the different Buddha images, the monks and nuns of Nipponzan Myohoji have a photograph of the founder of their order, Nichidatsu Fujii, who has now died.

supported. But through joining in this walk, the Buddhists met members of CND and also many Quakers – Christians who are members of the Society of Friends, a branch of the Church which is especially committed to peace, and whose members have refused to fight in times of war. This friendship with other people who were working for peace encouraged them, and gave them many useful contacts. They believe that this sort of demonstration is most essential – to awaken people to the need to help prevent the madness of nuclear war.

At Milton Keynes, the Buddhists are building a temple near the peace pagoda. Here people may come to join in Buddhist worship, or to meet and talk with the monks and nuns.

In front of Buddhist shrines belonging to Nipponzan Myohoji are the words NAMU MYOHO RENGE KYO. These words are chanted as part of their worship. There is no simple way to translate them, but they refer to the buddha nature which is within everyone, and which can lead a person towards peace. The monks use these same words when they greet people, putting their hands together as a sign of respect.

They are also laying out a traditional Japanese garden. This too is a way of expressing the Buddhist idea of inner peace – seeing the beauty and order in the garden can help

He does not work for money, but is supported by the gifts of those who come to worship at the temple, or who want to support the work of the Buddhist community. In this way, he is freed from worries about earning a living, and is able to give himself to his work as a monk.

This does not mean that he does not work as hard as other people. Monks and nuns have to do practical work around the temple and its surroundings – cooking, cleaning and building – as well as the religious duties of leading worship and teaching people about Buddhism.

a person to find a sense of beauty, peace and order within himself or herself.

Some of the work on this garden is being done by young people from all over Europe, who come to take part in Quaker peace camps at the temple. This is another example of peace – people of different religions working together.

In this and similar ways, the Buddhist monks and nuns of Nipponzan Myohoji try to create an atmosphere in which people may learn the meaning of peace for themselves, and therefore be more able to live at peace with others. By doing this, they hope that peace will spread worldwide, and will eventually remove the danger of war.

Over to you

1 Look at the photograph of the shopping street in Japan and then at the Japanese garden.
   ● Make a list of words describing each one.
   ● Why do you think a Japanese Buddhist might want to create a garden like this near a temple?

2 Japan had been at war before the dropping of the atomic bomb on Hiroshima, and many thousands of people had been killed. What do you think was so special about the atomic bomb that it made Nichidatsu Fujii decide to start his campaign for peace?

3 Buddhist pagodas are designed to give people a feeling of peace and holiness when they look at them. Can you think of any building you have seen which – because of its size or beauty – has made you feel that it is rather special? Describe it, and the feelings it gave you.

Address for further information:

Nipponzan Myohoji Peace Pagoda
Willen
Milton Keynes   MK15 0BA

Cicely Saunders

CARING FOR THOSE WHO ARE COMING TO THE END OF THEIR LIVES

66 *You need to care for the whole person, not just attend to their needs.* 99

Dame Cicely Saunders is Founder and Chairman of St Christopher's Hospice, in South London, and has worked for many years to promote the care of those who are dying. She has done this both through the use of drugs and nursing care, to enable people to be as comfortable, pain free and active as possible, and also by creating a peaceful and relaxed atmosphere in which the seriously ill can enjoy the final phase of their lives. She has shown that the end of life can be a precious time, both for the person who is dying and for his or her family and friends.

66 *Whenever you come up against a brick wall in life, there is often a door somewhere to one side which allows you to continue along your chosen path.* 99

When she came to leave school, Cicely Saunders thought she would like to become a nurse, but her family didn't think that would be suitable for her, and persuaded her that she should go to university. So she went to Oxford to read Philosophy, Politics and Economics.

While she was there, the Second World War started, and she felt that she should do something practical. She left Oxford to follow up her original wish to train as a nurse in St Thomas's Hospital in London.

In 1944, when she had qualified as a nurse, she found that she had back trouble. She was told that she would have to give up nursing because she would not be able to lift patients, or do other heavy work.

Although she was disappointed about this, she was determined to find some other way of working within the hospital world. So, instead of being a nurse, she trained to be a medical social worker – a person who helps people to sort out their problems and their plans, and sees that both patients and their relatives have what they need to cope with the practical problems of living with illness.

David Tasma said:

❝ *I'll be a window in your home.* **❞**

Controlling pain by giving exactly the right amount of drugs is an important part of caring for those who are seriously ill.

While working as a medical social worker, she met one particular patient, called David Tasma. He was young and dying. He was also a very lonely person, and felt that much of his life had been wasted. As she got to know him, she realised just how important it is for all those who work in hospital, the doctors and the nurses, to understand the whole person who comes to be their patient, and not just the medical problem of their illness.

Cicely Saunders realised that understanding and friendship were that two most important things to share with those who are seriously ill. One day David Tasma said, "I want what is in your mind and in your heart." For him, understanding and friendship were like a window being opened, a window into his heart, a window through which he could see life in a new way. She became very fond of him, and decided that she wanted to help all those who were dying, and to make it her life's work.

She spoke to him about setting up a home for those who were dying, and he arranged to leave her some money as a contribution towards the building.

Cicely Saunders started working as a voluntary sister in St Luke's Hospital, Bayswater, a home for the dying. While she was there, a doctor told her that, if she was serious about helping to improve the quality of care for those who were dying, the best way to do it was to become a doctor.

Although she was older than the other students, she went to St Thomas's Hospital Medical School, and qualified as a doctor in 1957. She received a scholarship to do research into the control of pain in those who were dying, and did this work based at St Mary's Hospital, Paddington. She also worked at St Joseph's Hospice, which was run by Christian nuns, and at St Luke's Hospital.

She learned how to control pain by the skilful use of drugs, and found that it was important to give a person what drugs he or she needed regularly, well before any pain started. Patients who knew that they would have enough drugs and would not have to fear pain became far less tense and anxious. They knew that they would not be left waiting for the next dose of medicine in order to feel comfortable. They also became more hopeful about their lives and less depressed about their illness.

In 1959 Cicely Saunders started raising funds from charitable trusts and individual people in order to set up her hospice – a place of medical care for those who were

*Christians have always been
concerned to help those who
are sick. In the Middle Ages,
monks used to provide resting
places for travellers. They
called them 'hospices' from a
Latin word* hospes, *meaning
'guest'. They offered their
guests food, shelter and
medical care. In modern
times, the word 'hospice' is
used for places that care for
those who are seriously ill.*

coming to the end of their lives. St Christopher's Hospice was completed in 1967, and it had a window dedicated to David Tasma, who had given her the very first contribution towards the building, twenty years earlier.

Cicely Saunders called her hospice 'St Christopher's' because, as a Christian, she believes that death is not the end of everything, but is a brief stopping place on a journey, as a person leaves this life and goes on to be with God. St Christopher is the patron saint of travellers.

Dame Cicely Saunders is often referred to as the founder of the modern hospice movement. This is because, following her work at St Christopher's, many other hospices have been set up in Britain and throughout the world. They all seek to put into practice her guidelines about the personal care and treatment of those who are seriously ill. In the years since St Christopher's was founded, there have been many improvements in the control of pain and the care of patients. Part of the work of the hospice is to research into this, and to share its findings with others.

St Christopher's Hospice

*"A bed is brought down to the
entrance, complete with a hot
water bottle to make the new
arrival feel comfortable and
welcomed. Matron greets
patients and their relatives,
and takes them up to the
ward, where they are
introduced to the other
patients and staff."*

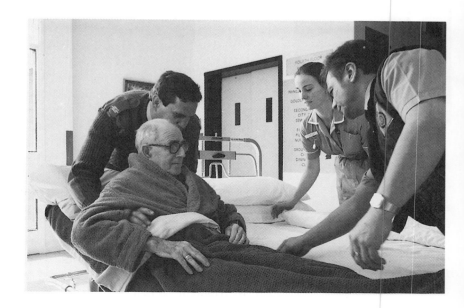

The hospice is cheerful and comfortable. Those who are ill are surrounded by friendly faces, by flowers and by reminders of their lives at home. There is a balcony, so that

66 *Here at St.
Christopher's we are like
a village, with people of
all ages mixing
together.* 99

patients can sit out in the sunshine, and wide corridors, so
that wheelchairs and beds can be moved about easily.

Part of the hospice is set aside for elderly people. They
have their own things around them, but can get help from
the hospice staff when they need it. There is also a
playgroup for the children of members of staff.

In St Christopher's there are sixty-two beds, and about
ninety nurses, along with the other staff and many
voluntary helpers. There is always someone around with
time to listen if a patient is alone and wants to talk. Before
St Christopher's and other hospices started to care for
those who were dying, they would have stayed in busy
general hospitals, if they could not be looked after at home.
Doctors had little time to spare for them, and some felt that
they had failed their patients if they could not cure them of
their illnesses.

Hospices are very different from general hospitals.
Doctors and nurses have plenty of time to help their
patients, to talk with them, listen to their problems, and
help their families and friends to cope with the sadness of
knowing that they are soon to lose someone dear to them.

66 *It's not like a
hospital where
everything is done in a
great rush. Here we all
have plenty of time to
talk to one another and
to create a feeling of
welcome.* 99

Joan – *by Dame Cicely Saunders*

Joan was 29 and her 4 children aged from 4–13 when she first met the St Christopher's Hospice Team. The hospital which had been treating her cancer had found that in spite of all their efforts it was spreading and becoming very painful and they asked the Hospice to control her pain and help her to live as well as she could for the rest of her life.

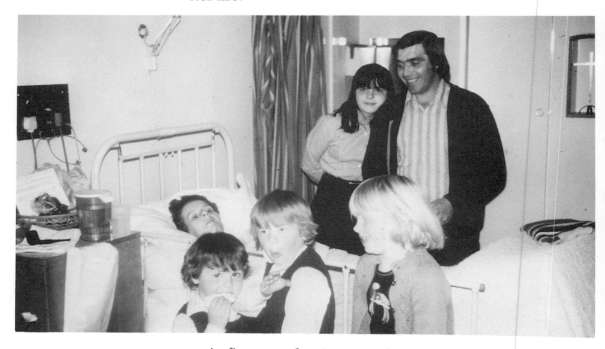

Joan's family round her bed.

At first, good pain control meant that she was mostly at home and she made a brave fight to struggle on, but for her last months the Hospice gave her a room to herself where her family could visit as much as they liked. Altogether, she had well over a year in which her pain was tackled and controlled and she felt in charge of all that happened. Her family were in and out and made it home and gradually Joan and her husband Alan talked through all that was happening and she helped him to plan the life of the family that she knew she would not see grow up. They were all helped by the care and friendship of the girl next door, whom Alan later married happily.

Joan kept alert and cheerful to the end of her life, even though she gradually had to give up walking and finally even sitting out in a chair. Her bedside was a centre of attention for them all.

Alan wrote to the Hospice afterwards 'Joan accepted what life gave her and with the skill and loving care of the Hospice, coupled with her determination, gave her an extra year of life – this chapter of my life has been filled with loving care and kindness which I have never come across in life before.'

The first visit back — a year later.

For several years the whole family came back visiting because they felt they wanted to see the Hospice again and we were happy to see them growing up, feeling secure even as they faced the loss of their mother. Now, over 10 years later, they write and keep in touch.

Still coming back to see us several years later.

Many people are completely cured of cancer. For others it is controlled by treatment so that they can live normal lives for long periods. But in some, like Joan, it continues to advance and many of them need special care to make them comfortable.

St Christopher's Hospice has always encouraged people to remain in their own homes for as long as possible, if that is what they want. Teams of nurses go out to care for the ill in their homes, and they are reassured that there will be a place for them in the hospice if they or their relatives cannot cope any more. Social workers arrange grants for those in special need, and also for a telephone to be installed, if people don't already have one. This is important so that they can keep in touch with the hospice.

There is also a club for those whose relatives have died in St Christoper's. It is called the Pilgrim Club, and its members meet once a month to talk about their problems and grief, and all their feelings about being bereaved. Some relatives find that they want to help others, and come back to St Christopher's as voluntary helpers in the hospice.

Some of the cost of beds in hospices is paid for by the National Health Service, but most comes from money donated by people and institutions who want to help with this work. In St Christoper's only one third of the cost of running the hospice is provided by the National Health Service, and the rest comes from gifts. Sometimes schools run charity events to raise money for the hospice, and there is an organisation – the Friends of St Christopher's – which raises money and helps in many other ways as well.

"When someone has a birthday or a wedding anniversary, we have a party. Friends and relatives of those who are ill can visit at any time. Sometimes even pet animals have been brought into St Christopher's so that their owners can see and enjoy time with them."

The care of those who are seriously ill

If you have an accident and break your arm, there is a sudden pain. Although it feels terrible at the time, you know that it will soon be over. It is different if you have a serious illness. People who are ill may suffer in four different ways, and may need help to overcome each of them.

1 It hurts!

When you are ill, parts of your body may hurt or ache. This is the most common kind of pain, and it can be controlled by drugs. A person is given exactly the right amount of a specially prepared mixture of drugs, to make sure that he or she is kept free of pain, but is not made too drowsy. It is also important to give careful nursing care, to make sure that the person is as comfortable as possible. Once free from pain, he or she can start to enjoy life again, and take an interest in things.

2 I want to be in control!

People like to be in charge of their own lives. They like to decide what to do and when to do it. Because of this, they may feel terribly helpless when illness stops them from getting about or doing their normal work. They may suddenly feel cut off from other people – everyone else can go out and enjoy themselves, but not them! This can be a real cause of suffering. Those who are seriously ill need people around them who can find time to talk with them, to share things – perhaps simply to have a cup of tea together. This reminds those who are ill that they are still loved and valued, even though they may feel helpless because of their illness.

3 How will my family cope without me?

When people are ill, and especially if they know that they do not have long to live, they may worry about how their families are going to cope without them. Everyone needs practical help and advice at this time. A seriously ill person can relax more, and enjoy time with his or her relatives and friends, once he or she knows that they are going to be able to manage afterwards.

Some people become angry.

> ❝ It's perfectly all right to be angry – but don't be angry with other people, it's not their fault! Don't be angry with yourself; it's not your fault either, and that will only make you depressed. Try to be angry with the situation, because it's so unfair! Death is an outrage, especially for the young. ❞

> ❝ If you're angry like that, you so often find that God is beside you. He is equally angry at the situation, and he is the one who can give you the strength to get through it and find your way to an answer. ❞

4 What's the point?

People need to find some sense of purpose and meaning in their lives. "What's it all been for?" a depressed person may ask, looking back on his or her life. This is a kind of spiritual pain. For some people, this will be a time for them to express what their lives are about through their religion. At St Christopher's, there are Christian prayers in the wards of the hospice, and there are services in the chapel. Nobody is forced to take part in religious worship, but many find it comforting. Those who do not belong to one of the world religions may want time to talk and reflect about what they have done with their lives. Just as, at the end of a school term, or a holiday, you may want to look back and think about what you have done, so a person who knows that his or her life is nearly over will look back – sometimes with happiness and sometimes with regret. It can be a time to say "thank you" or "sorry", or sometimes to tell people exactly what you think of them!

All of these things are forms of pain, and they can be helped if people are willing to give time to listen to what the ill person has to say, and to help him or her to come to terms with the illness. This is not just medical care for the bit of the body that has become ill, but care for the whole person, along with his or her family and friends as well. People need to feel that they matter, to know that people will be honest and friendly with them, and to appreciate the good things in life that they can enjoy, even if they are limited in what they can do. They can only do that if they feel that they are cared for and respected, just as they are.

> 66 *When you're really enjoying yourself, time can seem to stand still. When you're bored, it drags. A hospice can offer a very special kind of time – time to enjoy friends and family; time to think about the important things of life; time to be quiet, or time to talk. People in a hospice are surrounded by staff and helpers who have time to listen, and time to give extra care when it is needed.* 99

Would you want to know?

Many people try not to think about death. They may see people being killed on the television, but don't think it will ever happen to them. Yet the only thing that we all have in common is that one day we will die. We cannot run away from death, it is a natural part of life.

Some people seem to prefer not to know if they are dying. They may realise what is happening, but don't want to talk about it. Others may ask whether or not they are going to recover from their illness. Some people are told by a doctor that they may not have very long to live – but only

Cicely Saunders has received many awards and honours, and in 1980 she was made a Dame of the British Empire (which means that her official title is Dame Cicely Saunders), in recognition of her work in leading the way towards better care for the dying.

when they really want to know, and seem to be ready to know.

As long as they know that they are going to be well looked after, and that they will be kept free from pain, some people find that it is quite a relief to know the truth, especially if they have been worried and uncertain about their illness and its treatment.

Cicely Saunders, and the other people who work in the hospice movement, have shown that the end of life can be an important time for those who are dying and for their relatives. By aiming to keep them free from pain, and by providing them with the very best in care, they allow them to use the time they have left. St Christopher's Hospice is not a gloomy place – it is bright and cheerful, for the people there are helping the seriously ill to carry on fulfilling their lives, right up to the end.

Over to you

1 Some people, when they know that they are coming towards the end of their life, want to think back over all that they have done. They may want to think of their childhood, of how things were when their life began.
   ● Why do you think they might want to do this?
   ● How best could you help them to do so?

2 Try to remember a situation in which you have been ill (not necessarily a serious illness – flu, perhaps).
   ● What did you find helped you most while you were ill?
   ● Who looked after you? What did they do for you that made you feel better while waiting for the illness to pass?
   ● Make a list of the things that a seriously ill person might want in a hospice. Put them in what you believe might be their order of importance, and then compare your list with the one drawn up by another pupil.

3 Doctors at a general hospital sometimes find it hard to give the time and attention that the dying person may need.
   ● Why do you think that this is the case?
   ● Why might some doctors find it difficult to talk to their patients about the seriousness of their illness, and the fact that they are not going to recover from it? (Imagine you are a doctor – what might go through your mind as you talk to a patient whom you cannot cure?)

Address for further information:

St Christopher's
Hospice
51/59 Lawrie Park Road
Sydenham
London   SE26 6DZ

St Christopher's provides lists of books for pupils and teachers on the issues of death and care of the dying.

Akhandadhi das

WORKING TO PROMOTE HAPPINESS THROUGH KRISHNA CONSCIOUSNESS

> 66 *We believe God is a person; the Supreme Person. He is known by many names, and one of these is Krishna, which means 'the all attractive'. God has features that make him attractive to everyone. He has a very loving, caring nature, and we can find our greatest happiness by joining ourselves with him through devotion.* 99

You're telling us about life after death, but what about life before birth?

I hadn't thought of that.

Martin Fleming set aside the prospect of a career as an architect in order to join the International Society for Krishna Consciousness. Now, as Akhandadhi das, he is temple president at the Krishna Consciousness movement's centre at Bhaktivedanta Manor, Hertfordshire. As a devotee of Krishna, he has found a way of life that gives him great satisfaction, and also fulfils his long-standing ambition to help others, through adding to the spiritual quality of life. His responsibilities include the practical and financial side of running the temple and its activities, and also the care and spiritual direction of those who live there or come to worship.

He is convinced that society is going through a period of change – that people are becoming more sensitive and thoughtful – and he has a feeling that, in the twenty-first century, many more people will have the kind of lifestyle and values that he has found in Krishna Consciousness.

Martin Fleming was born in Belfast in 1954. His family were Protestant Christians, and belonged to the Presbyterian Church. As well as attending church services, their social life and friendships all centred on the church. Martin soon realised that religion was not just to do with the occasional act of worship, but something you should live by every day.

In his teenage years, he went through a stage when he would argue against the things that he was taught to believe at church, although he had a strong conviction that there was some sort of spiritual reality, and continued to believe in God. At an early age he started asking his Bible Class teacher difficult questions.

> ❝ From a very early age I thought that I would do something in the spiritual line, but I never really saw myself as a priest. I was attracted by the idea of a simple life, living as part of a spiritual community, where each person could offer his or her own special abilities. ❞

Martin was also unhappy about the direction in which society seemed to be going.

> ❝ I felt that the 'consumer society', and the drive for a life based on material comforts, was just not healthy. It didn't seem to be making people happy, and I didn't like the selfishness that it involved. ❞

> ❝ Isn't it wonderful what they are able to do? It must be rather nice to live a simple, spiritual life like that." ❞

Although he saw things he liked in the spiritual life of the Church, he had a feeling that there had to be something more – some other way of looking at religious belief. He started reading books on Indian philosophy, and immediately felt at home with the ideas he found there. He was attracted by the idea of meditation, and felt convinced that it was possible to know far more about God than most people supposed, although he saw that it would take a bit more effort to do so.

His first contact with Krishna Consciousness was in 1969. The Hare Krishna mantra (religious chant) was in the pop charts, and he remembers seeing the devotees (followers of Krishna Consciousness) on the television, walking in a procession and chanting. Krishna Consciousness was new to Britain then, and few people saw it as a serious religion to be followed. Martin envied its followers, but thought that he could never do anything like that himself.

Then, one Sunday while he was at home revising for his A levels, there came a knock at the door. It was a Krishna Consciousness devotee, distributing literature. They talked together, and Martin was amazed to find that he did not disagree with anything the devotee said. His ideas seemed to make sense of all that Martin himself had been thinking, and this led him to read more about the devotee's beliefs.

He went to Bristol University to study architecture, but had no intention of spending his life designing office blocks. He hoped that he would find out how to make people happy through his work, but soon discovered that happiness did not depend on having a nice house or environment. People could be unhappy, even if they lived in a really beautiful house. He and his fellow students studied town planning – but when they looked at every scheme, they found that there were reasons why it would not work. It became clear to him that the basic problem was so-called human nature – the selfishness within everyone.

While at university, he met devotees and bought books on Krishna Consciousness. He was taking it more seriously, thinking about it very carefully, and trying to see how it applied to the world. But when he discussed it with friends, he found himself getting into arguments with them. It was a philosophy that challenged their whole attitude to life and the values by which they lived.

Chanting

Followers of Krishna Consciousness have a 'mantra' – a set of words which they chant over and over again in their worship. By repeating two of the names for God (Krishna and Rama), this becomes a form of meditation in which they focus their minds on God, and recognise that he is present with them in a loving way.

This was Martin Fleming's early experience of chanting:

Hare Krishna
Hare Krishna
Krishna, Krishna
Hare Hare
Hare Rama
Hare Rama
Rama, Rama
Hare Hare.

A mantra is meant to free the mind from all anxiety. The Hare Krishna maha(great)-mantra is perhaps the most important mantra of the ancient religion of India.

66 *I thought, 'We can't do anything unless we can change human nature. To give people happiness, we will have to offer them something internal, something spiritual.'* 99

66 *I'm usually a happy sort of person. I've always felt that God is in control and that somehow everything will work out. But there have been times when I would think*

I've got problems, and I can't see a way out, no matter which way I go over them.

So then I'd sit down and say to myself

Now, for the next fifteen minutes I'm not going to think about problems – I'm just going to chant.

When you begin to chant seriously, it seems very strange at first. But chanting the mantra does not empty the mind; it focuses the mind on the sound vibration – the name for God. I don't think that meditation on anything other than God would be of any spiritual benefit. I found that, at the end of the fifteen or twenty minutes, my heart would just be singing, and I'd be telling myself

Why are you so happy? You have all these problems that you have not dealt with yet!

But I'd find that the problem seemed different in two ways after I'd been chanting. There might be a slight change in the circumstances (a miracle perhaps, or coincidence) but, at the same time, I would become detached from whatever I was wanting previously. We often have problems because we want something and can't get it. It's like a situation where you see that some doors are closed to you; but when you stand back and look again, you see that going through those doors may not necessarily lead to what you wanted – and there are other doors open to you instead. In this way, things that had seemed a problem turned out to be an advantage. 99

Although he wasn't chanting in this way very often, Martin Fleming found that it helped him a great deal, and it made him more convinced about his Krishna Consciousness. Although continuing to study architecture, he realised that his aims were only going to be satisfied through the spiritual path.

Devotees go out into the streets to chant their mantra. In this way they hope to show people something of the attractiveness of Krishna Consciousness. They may also offer books about Krishna Consciousness in exchange for a donation. This both spreads the message about their religion and also helps to raise funds to publish more books.

His decision

In the summer of 1975, at the end of the university term, he suddenly felt that the time had come to make the change. He gave his things away to his friends, told the university that he wouldn't be coming back, and wrote a letter to his parents, telling them what he was doing. Then he set off to Bhaktivedanta Manor. He had no idea what temple life would be like, but he knew that the devotees he had met were nice people, and that he could get on with them.

If you've got a real plan to do something, do it now!

Some of his friends just couldn't understand it, and his parents found it very difficult to accept. They felt that something terrible must have happened to him, and that he had become like a different person. Only after some years – and especially when he had married and then presented them with a grandchild – did they come to accept and appreciate his new way of life, and realise that it was one that gave him great satisfaction.

The International Society for Krishna Consciousness

Martin Fleming became known as Akhandadhi das. Akhanda means 'unbroken', dhi means 'intelligence' or 'meditation' and das means 'servant'. Das is added to the names of all devotees; they are to serve God and one another. So, Akhandadhi means 'one whose thoughts are always fixed on God', and Akhandadhi das is the servant of such a person.

While still a young married man, Bhaktivedanta Swami Prabhupada had been asked by his spiritual teacher to go to the West and teach people about Krishna – one of the most important of the Hindu gods – but it was only years later, at the age of seventy, that he had the chance to leave India. He arrived in America in 1965 with nothing, but he gave classes in meditation, and gradually gathered a group of followers. It was a time when many people, especially the young, were becoming dissatisfied with all the material things that their lives seemed to offer them. They were looking for something to give them a sense of peace and inner freedom.

Krishna Consciousness arrived in Britain in 1969, and in 1973 established its headquarters at Bhaktivedanta Manor in Hertfordshire, a large house given to the movement by George Harrison (of the Beatles), who had become a follower of Krishna Consciousness.

Those who are dedicated to Krishna Consciousness are called 'devotees'. There are about 400 full-time devotees in Britain, either living in the temples, or closely associated with them. Several thousand others practise Krishna Consciousness at home, making it part of their daily lives, while continuing their ordinary work and family responsibilities. There are about 100,000 people, many from the Asian community in Britain, who feel involved with the movement – they might come to the temple for a festival or make a contribution.

Those who want to become full-time devotees go through a period of preparation. They live and work in a temple for three months, to see if they like the life and are happy to live with the other devotees, and to learn more about Krishna Consciousness.

After following the religion for at least a year, a devotee may wish to take initiation. At this time, he or she receives a new name (in Sanskrit, the traditional religious language of India). This marks the beginning of his or her new life as a servant of God.

Those who have gone through this stage, and are growing and developing spiritually, then go through another ceremony. This is called the Brahmin Initiation. In

Bhaktivedanta Manor in
Hertfordshire.

" *I'm responsible for
the teaching that all the
students receive, and for
making sure that there is
a nice spiritual
atmosphere. I also spend
time dealing with
individuals –
counselling them about
their personal
needs.* "

Krishna Consciousness, a Brahmin is a person who has
become qualified as a spiritual teacher or priest. At a
Brahmin Initiation, a devotee is given a sacred thread,
which is worn over one shoulder and across the body. He
or she is also given a special mantra to chant.

Finally, there are a few men who – when they are older,
and have completed their family responsibilities – take
vows of poverty (having no personal goods), celibacy
(having no sexual partners) and commitment to preaching
and teaching Krishna Consciousness. A man who reaches
this stage is called a Sannyasi.

The work of a temple president

The president is in charge of running a temple, and he has
responsibility for everything that happens – whether it is
spiritual, personal, financial, or to do with the organisation
of work and preaching. He has to make sure that the
temple raises enough money to support itself, and that the
rules of their religion and the standards of worship
expected of Krishna Consciousness centres are kept up.

> *I feel very satisfied in the whole range of my activities. I'm doing far more things now than I would if I'd been an architect, or something like that. I'm also working more closely with people, and trying to help them be happy.*

> *Traditionally, there is a period in the morning, which starts an hour and a half before sunrise, which is considered the best time for spiritual practice. It is a time when everything is so peaceful and calm, and the mind is settled.*

> *Most people live with their lives upside down; they get up at the last minute and have to face the world before their minds are prepared for it.*

The temple president advises devotees on marriage – and although he does not arrange the marriage (in the sense of actually choosing partners), he will interview a couple who are thinking about marriage, and will help them to understand the responsibilities of family life.

He also has to balance the books – accounts have to be submitted, and the Charity Commission has to be satisfied that the organisation is operating properly because it is registered as a charity. Most of the money needed to run the temples comes in the form of donations from devotees in the congregation.

The life of a devotee

A regular pattern of life is important for peace of mind. A person who rushes around, doing different things each day, will find that it is impossible to practise meditation or proper study. A routine is useful for achieving anything, and those who live in temples therefore follow a disciplined lifestyle.

Devotees get up at 4 a.m. and take a shower. They then spend two hours in chanting and worship. At 6 a.m. there is time for study. The most important Hindu scripture for devotees is the Bhagavad Gita. This teaches about Krishna and the way of life that is based on devotion to him, and is taken as the basis of Krishna Consciousness. After breakfast, devotees do practical work around the temple, cooking and cleaning. Some go out from the temple to teach others about the religion. Many families attend the temple for the morning ceremonies and classes, but then go to work because the temple itself cannot generally provide an income for all the families who live in it.

The day is divided between times of devotion in the temple and practical work. Evenings are spent in worship and study. Everyone goes to bed early, so that they are awake and fresh for their early morning start. Although a programme like this may sound rather solemn, it is not really like that at all, and temples have a relaxed atmosphere, in which devotees and their families can enjoy themselves.

Devotees of Krishna Consciousness wear loose-fitting, Indian-style clothes. They claim that these are comfortable and more suitable for meditation than tight-fitting Western styles.

Devotees do not smoke, or drink alcohol or coffee. They are vegetarian – partly because they (like other Hindus) do not think it is right to kill animals for food, and partly because everything they eat is first offered to Krishna in the temple, and in the Gita it says that he should be offered only milk and vegetarian foods.

All this may sound as if the devotee is giving up a great deal – but he or she may not see it that way. Akhandadhi and others say that they are very satisfied with their way of life. They claim to have found a sense of peace and spiritual satisfaction in doing this, which they could not find in the way they were living before joining Krishna Consciousness.

Akhandadhi das is optimistic about the future. He thinks that more and more people in Western society are realising that true happiness is not found in the number of things they own, or the success of their careers. Instead, they are starting to look for satisfaction in more spiritual things – a sense of peace and inner happiness. He has found his way to these things through Krishna Consciousness, and he is now *leading the way*, by trying to teach others how to enjoy the worship of Krishna.

Most of the unmarried men, and those who work in the temple itself, shave their heads (all except for a small knot of hair at the back) as another sign that they are devoted to Krishna, and as a gesture of renunciation. Those who work outside the temple, mixing with people who are not devotees, tend not to shave their heads.

66 *I don't shave my head because I have to do a lot of activities in the outside world. But it doesn't mean that I am any less devoted to Krishna.* **99**

Address for further information:

International Society for Krishna Consciousness
Bhaktivedanta Manor
Letchmore Heath
Watford
Hertfordshire   WD2 8EP

Over to you

1 Make a list of all the things you do in a day, and when you do them. Then compare your life with that of a Krishna devotee.
   ● Which do you prefer? Why?
   ● What would be the hardest thing for you in following the routine of temple life? Why?
   ● What, if anything, most appeals to you in the lifestyle of a Krishna devotee? Give your reasons.

2 Imagine that you have a friend who is thinking of taking the step that Martin Fleming took – leaving a career to join the Krishna Consciousness movement. Think about the issues that you would want to discuss with him or her. What would be the advantages and disadvantages of becoming a devotee? Act out, or write down, what you would want to say.

3 Do you think that all images point towards the same God? If so, does it matter what form of worship you choose to practise? Give your reasons.

Jean Vanier

HELPING THOSE WITH LEARNING DIFFICULTIES

66 *In a special way, for those of us called to live or work with very broken people, our purpose is to help them rise up and discover and exercise their own gifts, to discover their beauty and their capacity to love and to serve.* 99

Jean Vanier is the founder of L'Arche, a network of communities in which people with learning difficulties and those who care for them live together and learn from one another. He has also worked to establish 'Faith and Light', a movement which brings together people with learning difficulties along with their families and their friends, in order to share and celebrate together. The basis of his work is summarised in this extract from the Charter of the Communities of L'Arche:

> *We believe that each person, whatever the disability, has a unique and mysterious value. The person with a learning difficulty is a complete human being, and as such has the rights of every human being: the right to life, to care, to education and to work.*

When Jean Vanier left school, he decided to join the Navy. He went to Dartmouth Naval College and spent five years there, first in the Royal Navy and then in the Royal Canadian Navy (he is French Canadian). Then, in 1950, at the age of twenty-one, he went to France to study Philosophy and Theology (Religious Studies). He both studied and taught there for ten years, before returning to Canada to teach Philosophy at St Michael's College, University of Toronto.

In spite of his success as a teacher, he was still uncertain about what he should do with his life. He felt that he wanted something simpler, serving other people. To help him decide, he went back to France and then to Portugal, spending two years in study and prayer. He came to the conclusion that what he really wanted was to form some sort of Christian community – a place where people could share life together, a place that would go against the modern trend for people to be separated from one another.

Then, in 1964, he visited Father Thomas Philippe. He was an old friend of Jean Vanier's and the Catholic chaplain of Val Fleuri, a home for men with learning difficulties in Trosly, a village about 50 miles north of Paris. Jean Vanier knew nothing about the care of those with learning difficulties, but became concerned about the way in which they lived in large homes and hospitals. He felt that what they needed was simply security and friendship, and they could find that in a small community. So he bought a house in the village and took two young men – Raphael and Philippe – from the mental hospital to live with him. His life was completely changed – from being a popular university teacher, he now spent his time caring for these two men.

This was the start of a community which became called L'Arche. The following year, the director of Val Fleuri resigned, and Jean Vanier was invited to take his place, suddenly finding himself responsible for the lives of thirty men with learning difficulties.

Since that first house in Trosly, the idea of L'Arche has spread to many other places. There are now more than ninety L'Arche communities in twenty different countries, including six in Britain.

L'Arche means 'The Ark'. In the Old Testament, the Children of Israel had an Ark (a carved wooden box containing the laws by which they lived) which represented the presence of God among them. In the same way, Jean Vanier believed that God's presence would be found in the community of L'Arche.

A L'Arche home for men in Trosly, France, the village in which the first L'Arche community was formed.

85

Why do people have learning difficulties?

People may be born with a medical condition in which their mind is unable to control their body in the usual way, and which makes it more difficult for them to learn how to do things. Two of these conditions are Down's syndrome (sometimes called mongolism) and cerebral palsy (whose sufferers are sometimes called spastics). Some people have only mild disabilities, and are able to look after themselves and go out to work. Those who are severely disabled may not be able to speak, and may have little control over their physical movements.

In spite of these limitations, people with learning difficulties (who are sometimes referred to as being mentally handicapped) have and show feelings, just like anyone else. They can become angry and frustrated, and (because they may not be able to explain what the problem is, or what they need) they may sometimes express themselves in unusual or aggressive ways. They can also express love, and can do so very simply and beautifully – often finding it easier to show their emotions than those who, with greater mental control, are more likely to hide what they feel or be embarrassed.

Because of this, the first impression is that people who have learning difficulties are rather different from others. But later, as you get to know them and learn to communicate with them, you find that they are just the same as everyone else – they may sometimes show their feelings and thoughts differently.

Looking after a handicapped person at home can be demanding. Because of this, some parents find that they cannot cope with their child's learning difficulties, and he or she is then placed in a home, or may be fostered or adopted by another family. This leads to all sorts of hurt feelings – the parents may feel guilty that they cannot look after the person at home, and the child may feel that he or she is not wanted.

It is also difficult, in a world where people look for success, for parents to accept that their child is not going to succeed in the way that they might have hoped. They have to learn to accept his or her love, and to enjoy what he or she is able to do, without always comparing their child

> **"** *So many of us flee from people crying out in pain, people who are broken. We hide in a world of distraction and pleasure, or in 'things to do'.* **"**

> **"** *A whole system of competition and success . . . is based on the need to prove that 'I am better than you.'* **"**

with others who are more able. Sometimes children with learning difficulties may feel that they are a disappointment to their parents, and that too hurts.

How does L'Arche work?

The idea of L'Arche is that people with learning difficulties should not be set apart and be treated differently from others, but that they should live as part of a family. Each person is different, and some mentally handicapped people have great difficulty expressing themselves, but Jean Vanier wanted to show that they could still contribute to a family and to the village or town where they lived.

No two people have exactly the same kind of learning difficulties. Some are able to learn to look after themselves, but they need encouragement to do this, and they need to trust those who are caring for them. Part of the work of L'Arche is to help each person to have a 'project' – a goal to which that person is going to move, and a set of practical steps by which he or she can make progress. If a person with learning difficulties wants to become as independent as possible, he or she will need help at each stage, to learn how to cope with the pressures of life, and to master the problems one by one. Failure can mean loss of confidence, so each person has to take gradual steps, mastering one thing at a time, and gradually building up enough confidence to tackle new problems.

Living together in small groups, all members of the community share in the cooking and cleaning – each doing what he or she is able. In this way, everyone knows that they are important, and that they have something to contribute.

People with learning difficulties are referred to L'Arche by doctors, social workers or local hospitals. L'Arche communities generally take people from their own area, so that they can keep in touch with their families and friends after they join the community.

The most important thing about L'Arche is that the people with learning difficulties can become part of a family. They live in houses, along with the assistants who are there to help them. Unlike a hospital, where each member of staff has charge of a large number of patients, in a L'Arche community, there are almost the same number of assistants as those they are helping.

Some L'Arche communities only take adults with learning difficulties, others take children, and some also welcome those with physical disabilities. Most of the communities are funded by the government, and are able to survive because of money made available for the care of those in need. In other places, where there is no welfare money of this sort, the communities work to be self-supporting. In a L'Arche community in South India, for example, as well as growing food for themselves, they grow cashew nuts to be sold on the local market.

66 Can it be that the broken and neglected of our societies can become the source of peace and unity if people turn towards them as brothers and sisters, to welcome and serve them and to discover the gift that is theirs? 99

A family day at Lambeth. It is important for members of the community to stay in touch with families and friends.

66 Jesus will reveal to you that he is hidden in the poor, the weak, the lonely and the oppressed. 99

As a Christian, Jean Vanier believes that new life came to humankind because of the suffering of Jesus on the cross. In the same way, he believes that a special quality of life can come through the suffering of people with disabilities in our society.

About competition in society he says:

In richer countries life is dominated
by constant competition,
by the struggle for success and power.
In Canada I saw a sign in a classroom:
'It is a crime not to excel.'
Each one of us must succeed;
if we do not, we will have no status in society,
no work, no home.
We must win the prize or else be discarded.
So we learn to harden our hearts and fight and struggle
to be first,
to be better than anyone else.

Those who cannot make it fall by the wayside,
in sadness and anger.

66 *Joy springs from the wounds of brokenness.* 99

Meal times are a time of celebration, and those who sit round the table may hold hands and sing a grace together before they eat. The whole business of cooking and eating meals is important in L'Arche communities, as it is a means of bringing everyone together and sharing in simple tasks.

Imagine a situation where a group have a meal, but it is formal and a bit solemn. Then, afterwards, someone picks up a guitar and begins to sing. Gradually, the people around start to beat out the rhythm on anything that comes to hand – glasses and spoons. At once, faces start to light up, and there is a sense of festival. Only those who still feel too much anger inside themselves cannot join in. That is the sort of simple festival in which those with learning difficulties can share.

Jean Vanier argues that it is essential to have times of celebration, even among those who are poor and suffering.

It gives people the joy and strength to face their day-to-day hardships. He also says that there should be moments of silence in all celebrations, moments when people can remember those who cannot celebrate, those who are in despair or who are starving.

He points out the way in which we have become used to seeing suffering and war on the screens of our television sets, and we feel that there is nothing we can do. Often we may be tempted to turn away from it – change the channel for some entertainment which will help us to forget the sufferings of others.

Speaking about his work, Jean Vanier says:

> Much of my life over the last twenty years
> has been with men and women having a mental handicap
> I have seen and touched their pain:
> the terrible pain of being a disappointment to their parents.
> They feel weak, unable to cope with life
> which moves so fast around them.
> This feeling of not being wanted, just as they are,
> engenders a sense of guilt.
> They feel they have hurt their parents,
> because they were not a cause of joy
> but rather a source of worry and pain.
> So they think they are worthless, just a nuisance –
> maybe even evil.
> And from this loneliness arises anguish and confusion,
> an inner brokenness,
> no trust in themselves or in others.
> This in turn leads to violence,
> depression, disturbed behaviour,
> and so they are put aside even more,
> rejected.
> They sense that they belong nowhere and to no one.

But these feelings are not limited to those with learning difficulties. Vanier points out that they are shared by those who are old or out of work, immigrants, fragile and weak people, people with physical disabilities and long-term illness, people obsessed with eating, alcohol or drugs.

He also says that people who may appear on the outside to be successful and in charge of their lives may feel worthless inside, especially if they find that they cannot love and relate to the people around them.

One of Jean Vanier's most important ideas is that those who are poor and suffering not only have to be cared for, but they also need to be listened to, because they have something important to say. In their simple way, they may express a truth that a person who is intellectually gifted may overlook.

People with learning difficulties may be thought of as 'different', or 'mad', by those who call themselves 'normal', but Jean Vanier thinks that they may have a great deal to give to the world.

Jean Vanier believes that those who can accept their own suffering are able to share their lives in a way that other people cannot. Those who suffer should not be ignored by society; they are needed, and they have something important to contribute even if they are immobile, or are unable, through learning difficulties, to do the things that many people take for granted.

Jean Vanier shows that, when we love people, we listen to them, appreciate them and want them to live well and to grow. We forgive them for anything they have done against us, and want to share our lives with them. This kind of love is what he seeks in the communities of L'Arche.

An important part of loving people is to give them self-respect, and this can be helped by doing useful work. At Lambeth L'Arche there are workshops in which assistants and those with learning difficulties work together – some work with wood, making birdboxes, others create stoneware, or spend their time in rugmaking or weaving. Local people call into the shop at L'Arche to buy what they produce, and may place orders for work to be done. This is one of the ways in which a L'Arche community can keep in touch with local people.

Members of the community at Lambeth in the workshop where they produce stoneware.

Each day, the community members come from the different houses in which they live, and gather in the workshops. Whatever activity they take part in helps to earn money to run L'Arche, and also teaches skills that are of value. Instead of being 'looked after', those with learning difficulties are actually going out to work and producing something – just like other people in our society. It also gives them an opportunity to meet those who live in houses other than their own.

Working as an assistant

Generally, those who come to L'Arche communities as assistants find that they learn from the handicapped as well as being able to teach and help them. Those who arrive thinking that they are being extra good by offering to help others are likely to find that their motives are challenged! It does not take long for people with learning difficulties to sense if an assistant is honest and friendly.

The best helpers of the poor and the weak are those who are aware that there is a sense in which they themselves also know poverty and weakness – a person who never admits to being weak or wrong is hardly likely to be really sympathetic.

One problem for those who are helping people with learning difficulties is the temptation to do too much for them, instead of letting them find out how much they can do for themselves. But doing something for someone else may reinforce their sense of failure, while helping them to learn gives them a sense of their own value and achievement.

Sometimes assistants find that there is some opposition from their own families and friends to their life in L'Arche. Often it is assumed that they will go into a career with status and a good salary, or that they will do something glamorous with their life. The values at L'Arche are quite different, and that may come as a shock. Assistants may find great satisfaction, and learn a lot about themselves in the process, but that sort of thing may not always be understood by those outside the communities.

Assistants may also realise just how shallow were some of their old friendships, compared with those they now share. In spite of this, living and working in a small community can be tiring, and it is important that the assistants can get some time on their own, to rest and develop their own interests.

Some people work as assistants at L'Arche for just a few months and then leave. Although this may be a good experience for them, it can be unsettling for those they live with. Ideally, those who join L'Arche should hope to stay for at least one or two years. Many stay longer – about one-third of the assistants have worked at L'Arche for four or five years, and another third see it as something they intend to do for the rest of their lives.

> **66** *If you enter into a relationship with a lonely or suffering person you will discover something else: that it is you who will be healed. The broken person will reveal to you your own hurt and the hardness of your heart, but* also *how much* you *are loved. Thus the one you came to heal becomes your healer.* **99**

Faith and Light

Not every person with learning difficulties is able to live in a community like L'Arche, but all can benefit from meeting with others and sharing with them. Therefore, in 1971, Jean Vanier (along with Marie-Helene Mathieu) founded 'Faith and Light'. This is a network of communities of people who meet together from time to time, both the handicapped and the relatives and friends who care for them. There are now more than 600 of these communities all over the world. It started with a pilgrimage to Lourdes, the centre for healing in the South of France, which was attended by 12,000 people, one-third of whom had learning difficulties.

People who are poor, or who have disabilities, can sometimes be ignored in a society where success and good looks are rated important. Against this, Jean Vanier argues that Christians should be especially concerned with such people, and that there can be great joy in sharing life with them.

Contact addresses in Great Britain for L'Arche:

Little Ewell
Barfrestone
DOVER
Kent   CT15 7JJ

Braerannoch
13 Drummond Crescent
INVERNESS
IV2 4HD

L'Arche
15 Norwood High Street
LONDON
SE27

The Bridge
127 Prestcott Road
LIVERPOOL
L7 0LA

123 Longfield Road
BOGNOR REGIS
W. Sussex
PO21 1QD

119 Cradoc Close
BRECON
Powys
LD3 9UA

(Secretariat)
14 London Road
BECCLES
Suffolk
NR34 9NH
(Tel: 0502 715329)

Over to you

1 How do you celebrate special days? What do you enjoy most?
   ● Does celebration depend on spending a lot of money on food and drink?
   ● Why do you think that the poorest people in the world still seem to spend some of their time and limited resources on celebration?

2 We can learn a great deal from a person who has a lot of intellectual ability – information and ideas of all sorts.
   ● What sort of things can we learn from someone who has learning difficulties, which we might not learn otherwise?
   ● In what ways, other than by words, can we convey our thoughts and feelings to another person?

3 Imagine that you are trying to decide whether or not to become an assistant in a L'Arche community.
   ● Make a list of all the things that you find attractive in that way of life.
   ● List the objections that you think people might raise to your joining L'Arche.
   ● Which of these objections do you agree with? Which of them are either wrong, or outweighed by those things which attract you?

Leading the Way

VOLUME 2

Desmond Tutu	Campaigning against apartheid
Julia Neuberger	Looking at questions of morality, from embryo to adult
Dan Jones	Campaigning for prisoners of conscience
Sudarshan Abrol	Helping handicapped children
Bob Geldof	Feeding the world
Swee Chai Ang	Giving medical aid to Palestinians
Sangharakshita	Founding a new Buddhist movement in the West
Bruce Kent	Campaigning for peace
Jackie Pullinger	Helping the drug addicts of Hong Kong
Brother Roger	Listening to the young and the poor